Table of Contents – CONSTRUCT & CONSTRUCT2 2016/17 Edition

License Agreement

This book (the "Book") is a product provided by HobbyPRESS (being referred to as "HobbyPRESS" in this document), subject to your compliance with the terms and conditions set forth below. PLEASE READ THIS DOCUMENT CAREFULLY BEFORE ACCESSING OR USING THE BOOK. BY ACCESSING OR USING THE BOOK, YOU AGREE TO BE BOUND BY THE TERMS AND CONDITIONS SET FORTH BELOW. IF YOU DO NOT WISH TO BE BOUND BY THESE TERMS AND CONDITIONS, YOU MAY NOT ACCESS OR USE THE BOOK. HOBBYPRESS MAY MODIFY THIS AGREEMENT AT ANY TIME, AND SUCH MODIFICATIONS SHALL BE EFFECTIVE IMMEDIATELY UPON POSTING OF THE MODIFIED AGREEMENT ON THE CORPORATE SITE OF HOBBYPRESS. YOU AGREE TO REVIEW THE AGREEMENT PERIODICALLY TO BE AWARE OF SUCH MODIFICATIONS AND YOUR CONTINUED ACCESS OR USE OF THE BOOK SHALL BE DEEMED YOUR CONCLUSIVE ACCEPTANCE OF THE MODIFIED AGREEMENT.

Restrictions on Alteration
You may not modify the Book or create any derivative work of the Book or its accompanying documentation. Derivative works include but are not limited to translations.

Restrictions on Copying
You may not copy any part of the Book unless formal written authorization is obtained from us.

LIMITATION OF LIABILITY
HobbyPRESS will not be held liable for any advice or suggestions given in this book. If the reader wants to follow a suggestion, it is at his or her own discretion. Suggestions are only offered to help.

IN NO EVENT WILL HOBBYPRESS BE LIABLE FOR (I) ANY INCIDENTAL, CONSEQUENTIAL, OR INDIRECT DAMAGES (INCLUDING, BUT NOT LIMITED TO, DAMAGES FOR LOSS OF PROFITS, BUSINESS INTERRUPTION, LOSS OF PROGRAMS OR INFORMATION, AND THE LIKE) ARISING OUT OF THE USE OF OR INABILITY TO USE THE BOOK. EVEN IF HOBBYPRESS OR ITS AUTHORIZED REPRESENTATIVES HAVE BEEN ADVISED OF THE POSSIBILITY OF SUCH DAMAGES, OR (II) ANY CLAIM ATTRIBUTABLE TO ERRORS, OMISSIONS, OR OTHER INACCURACIES IN THE BOOK.

You agree to indemnify, defend and hold harmless HobbyPRESS, its officers, directors, employees, agents, licensors, suppliers and any third party information providers to the Book from and against all losses, expenses, damages and costs, including reasonable attorneys' fees, resulting from any violation of this Agreement (including negligent or wrongful conduct) by you or any other person using the Book.

Miscellaneous.

This Agreement shall all be governed and construed in accordance with the laws of Hong Kong applicable to agreements made and to be performed in Hong Kong. You agree that any legal action or proceeding between HobbyPRESS and you for any purpose concerning this Agreement or the parties' obligations hereunder shall be brought exclusively in a court of competent jurisdiction sitting in Hong Kong.

Preface

CONSTRUCT had revolutionized the world of open source 2D game creation, by providing easy drag-and-drop kind of interface for producing complex game logic, all without writing codes and scripts.

The goal of this book is to provide starters with rich technical information so the best decision and judgment can be exercised when creating 2D games through CONSTRUCT Classic and CONSTRUCT2. The current version of CONSTRUCT Classic is R1.2 which is released under the GPL. CONSTRUCT2 is different in licensing - it has a version for free personal use. A business license is required if you intend to make money through it.

Throughout this book we will simply refer to CONSTRUCT Classic as CONSTRUCT. On the other hand, we refer to CONSTRUCT2 as C2. This is not a step-by-step tutorial. This is also not a guide book kind of overview material. We place our focus on the practical side of game creation – practical tips and techniques one will definitely need when starting out a game project. We also tell exactly what can and cannot be done with Construct, and the kind of performance drawback that can be foreseen when the platform is not fed with the right inputs.

So, are you ready for the challenge?

Version Information

The current version of CONSTRUCT Classic is R1.2. This is different from the new CONSTRUCT 2, which is not released under the GPL.

CONSTRUCT 2 is not limited to Windows based creation. It can support mobile platforms and HTML5. For demo purpose we use R173 64 bit version in this book. The latest available version as of this latest edition is R236.

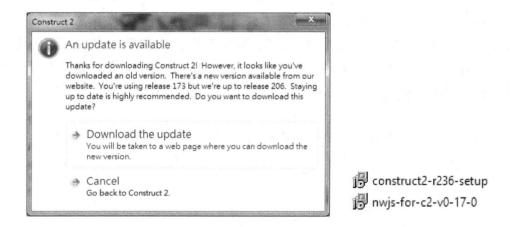

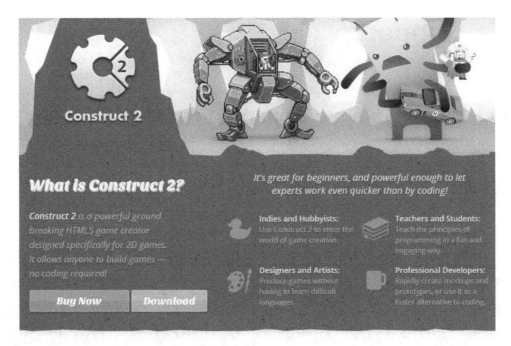

Whoever you are, Construct 2 has many features to help you!

Note that the installation of C2 is portable so you can take the installation to another computer without the need for reinstallation.

Copyright 2015. **The HobbyPRESS (Hong Kong)**. All rights reserved.

Basic Concepts

What kinds of game are Construct optimized for? Is

CONSTRUCT 3D capable?

CONSTRUCT is a development platform that can be used to create a wide range of 2D games and applications. What this means is that CONSTRUCT may simply NOT be optimized for any particular game type. Effective optimization usually requires specialization, but CONSTRUCT is more "general-purpose" oriented.

CONSTRUCT is primarily a 2D tool based on DirectX. It has an object type for displaying a 3D textured box but the effect is more of a scenic nature – it is for displaying a static 3D box object on the 2D layout.

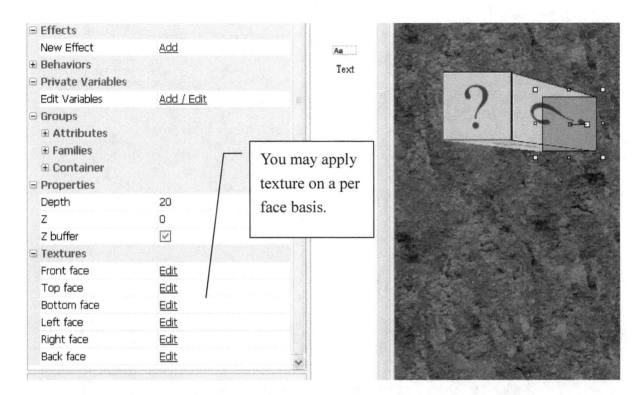

You may apply texture on a per face basis.

If you want to create a full blown 3D game, shop somewhere else. CONSTRUCT manipulates objects primarily as bitmaps. It does not yet have the capability of processing polygons the 3D style.

C2 is also primarily 2D. However, it really cares about the graphic card you use in your development system. Upon installation it will scan your system to detect any potential driver issues via its driver updater.

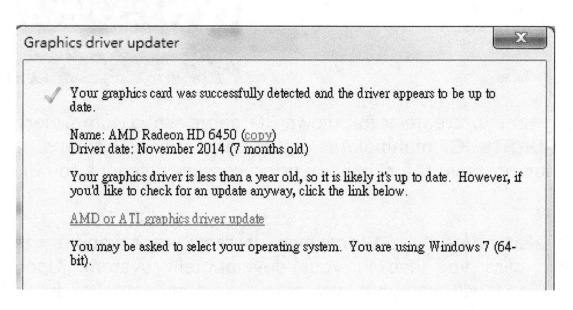

Is CONSTRUCT 64 bit? How about C2?

CONSTRUCT is primarily 32 bit. C2 has both 32 bit and 64 bit versions available:

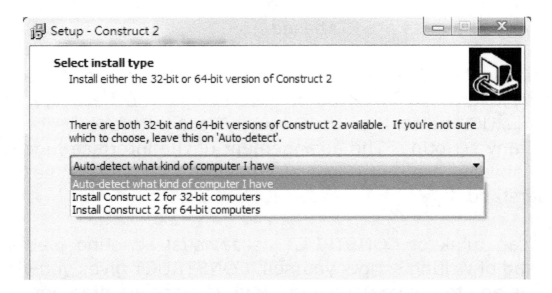

Why is CONSTRUCT a good choice for elementary game

creation? How about C2?

First of all, good game creation does not have to be 3D capable. Many good games are 2D based.

Secondly, the CONSTRUCT user interface (UI) is one of the best I have ever seen in terms of ease of use and flexibility. It is MUCH MUCH better than the Director/Flash interface. It does not need any scripting. The arrangement of the interface functions and objects are very logical, making things very easy to understand.

You can think of CONSTRUCT as a visual scripting platform. Instead of writing scripts yourself, CONSTRUCT gives you visual menus and forms so you can pick up choices via drag and drop and formulate scripts without writing codes. CONSTRUCT then generates the necessary scripts and commands for you transparently in the background. The game built runs primarily as EXE on Windows.

C2 further allows you to create games that run on platforms other than PC. In fact, C2 builds HTML5 games which can run on most platforms that support web browsing.

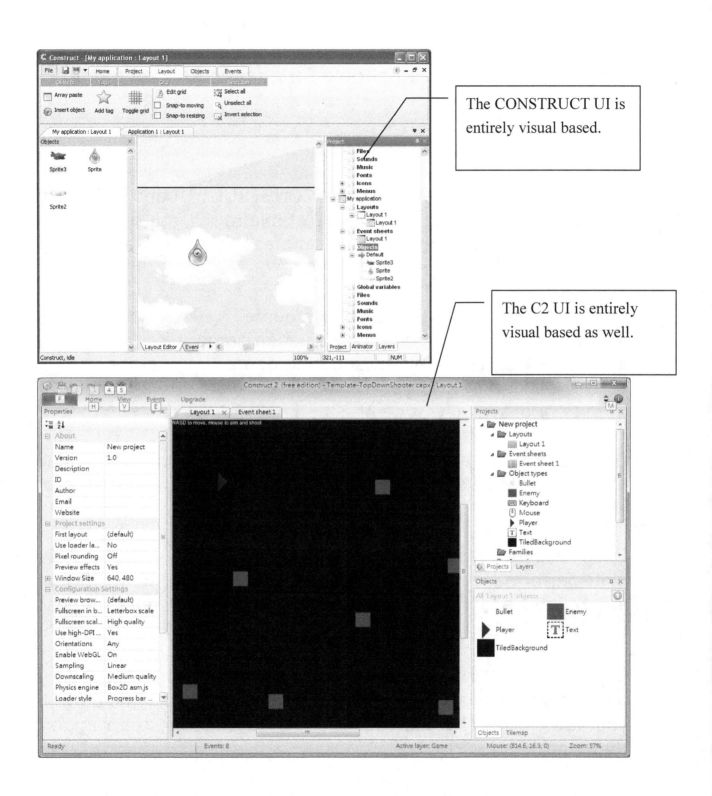

The CONSTRUCT UI is entirely visual based.

The C2 UI is entirely visual based as well.

Is CONSTRUCT a good choice for advanced level game creation? How about C2?

Based on my experience with the CONSTRUCT UI and the actual performance outcome, I am comfortable to tell you that certain types of 2D game can be professionally created with CONSTRUCT:

- the Candy Crush type of puzzle game
- the Mario Brothers type of 2D action game
- the R-Type/1942 kind of shooting game
- the YS kind of RPG game
- any bird-eye view type of action game

One good thing about CONSTRUCT is that it is a quite stable platform, that unknown weird runtime errors are not common at all.

Even though the game engine behind CONSTRUCT is NOT a very high performance one (graphic and effect-wise), it is efficient and reliable as long as you use it properly for the right purpose (in other words, you need to know its limitations).

Do note that CONSTRUCT does not offer very rich functions for graphic and special effect preparation. You need to come up with your own artworks and music using other tools, then import them into CONSTRUCT.

C2 offers many more advanced features. And the good thing about it is that it provides many templates for you to start with, making it easy to create advanced games:

Copyright 2015. **The HobbyPRESS (Hong Kong)**.

Do I need any special licenses for advanced game creation?

CONSTRUCT is released under the GNU General Public License (GPL) and nothing else. You are free to sell your game creations.

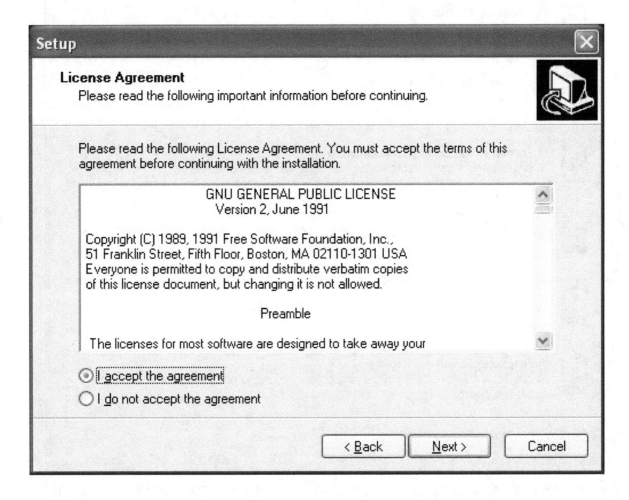

The GPL is a copyleft license, meaning that derived works can only be distributed under the same license terms. Simply put, the GPL grants the recipients of the software rights of the free software definition and uses copyleft to ensure the freedoms are preserved, even when the work is changed.

When you are using CONSTRUCT to create a game, you are not making deviations out of CONSTRUCT. You are simply creating works using CONSTRUCT as a foundation. Therefore, it is okay for you to create commercial games out of it. It is, however, NOT okay for you to create a commercial 3D game development platform out of it.

C2 has several licensing modes. If you are not planning to make a profit, the personal license is good enough. To sell games for profit you need to have a business license. There is also an educational license for training school and the like.

Is CONSTRUCT/C2 going to be easy (for me) if I have rich background in procedural programming languages like C and Pascal?

It is hard to say. The thing is, the CONSTRUCT/C2 engine is an event driven system, which is NOT procedural at all. It is not just about difference in language syntax. It is a totally different way of thinking.

Procedural thinking is usually top-down, with heavy focus on procedures and functions. An event driven system, on the other hand, consists of objects with different behaviors and properties, all interacting via events (which in turn would trigger actions).

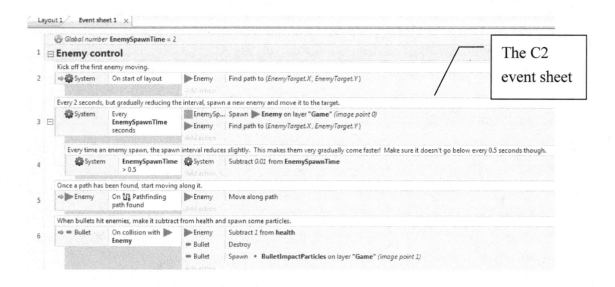

The C2 event sheet

Why would one prefer CONSTRUCT/C2 over GM Studio for game creation?

Game Maker GM Studio offers the Game Maker Language (GML) for scripting purpose. GML is sort of a scripting language that works and looks like something in between Pascal and C. GML is easier to learn than a true Object Oriented Language such as C++. At the same time it allows flexibility in coding. **To truly utilize the power of GM Studio one will for sure need to code.**

In contrast, CONSTRUCT/C2 's interactive interface is so powerful that the need for coding is minimal. CONSTRUCT does support scripting, but you shouldn't need to script much. Its major selling point is no-programming!

Why would one prefer CONSTRUCT over Clickteam Fusion

for game creation?

CONSTRUCT/C2 is highly similar to Clickteam Fusion in the way games can be built (so are the concepts behind their event driven mechanisms).

CONSTRUCT has very limited export options. However, C2 can export projects to a wide variety of platforms, although HTML5 is the main stream.

Can I master CONSTRUCT/C2 without understanding any

programming concept?

Frankly, no. Even though CONSTRUCT/C2 works as a visual tool, its core is no different from a traditional object oriented development system. It is fully event driven, and the only difference is that you may define the various event conditions and actions via a graphical/menu based interface.

To effectively plan how the different CONSTRUCT/C2 objects may interact, you'll need to fully understand the event-driven concept.

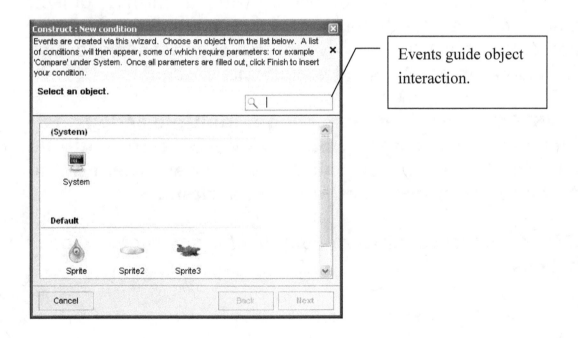

Events guide object interaction.

What is special about an event driven system? How does it work?

In an event driven environment, a program is structured in terms of events, with no preordered flow of control. Things do NOT start and proceed step by step. Instead, actions are associated with events, which will get invoked only when the corresponding event conditions are met (i.e. the event occurs). You do not know when these events will take place at design time. For example, object A has an action of shooting. This shooting action will not start UNLESS object B has an explosion. Whether or not object B will explode depends on whether the player can accurately hit object B with a missile object. Movement of the missile object is an action. The resulting collision (with object B) is an event. This event can trigger two sets of action: object B explodes and object A shoots.

In CONSTRUCT, an event can trigger multiple actions. For an event to "take place", you can even specify multiple conditions. Just keep in mind, you always define the conditions first prior to defining the actions.

CONSTRUCT provides a wizard type tool for defining conditions and actions:

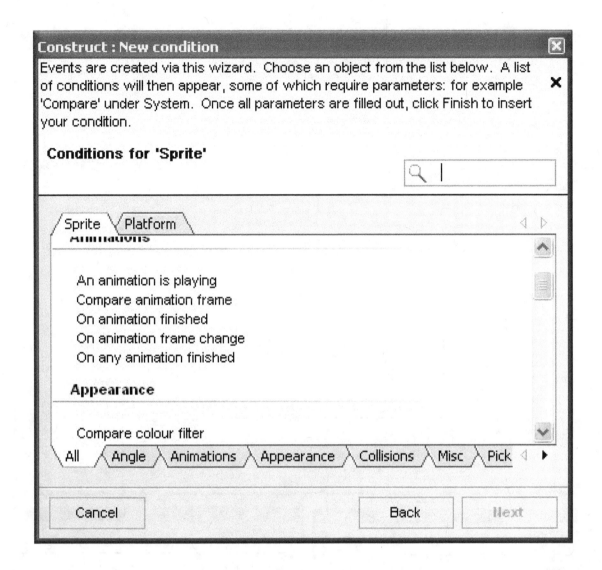

CONSTRUCT is event driven. It is also object oriented. Every item that shows up in the game is an object. Every object has a set of properties which represent the object's unique characteristics. They can be predefined, and some may even be manipulated at runtime through event triggered actions.

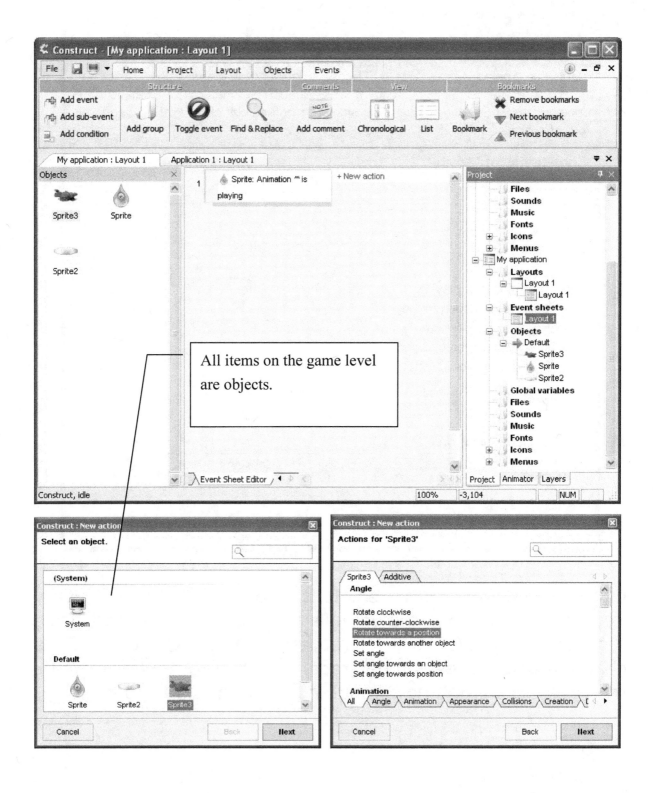

All items on the game level are objects.

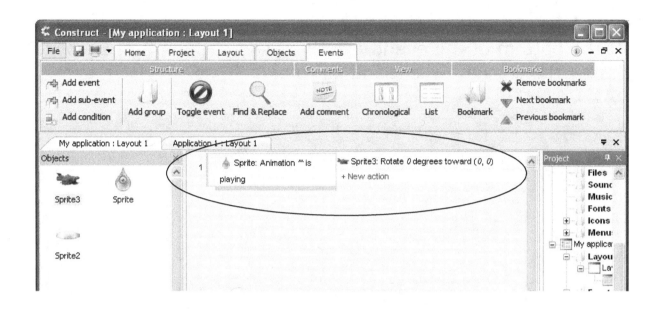

With C2, you can right click on the layout and choose Edit event sheet to invoke the Event Sheet.

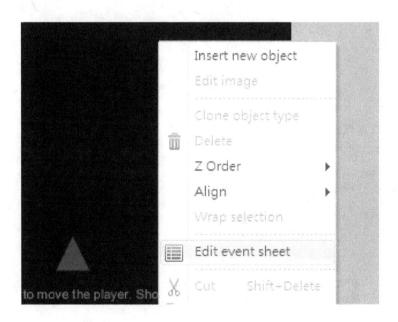

At the bottom of the event sheet you can click on Add Event to start writing a new event and its rules/actions.

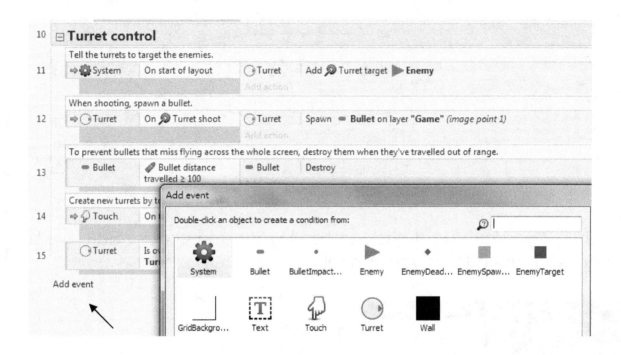

Then you pick an object for testing a condition:

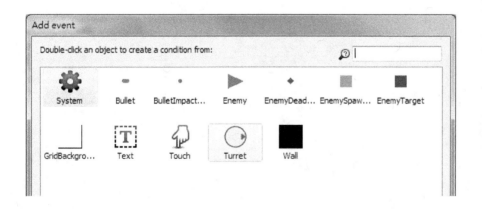

Then you pick a relevant event condition from the list:

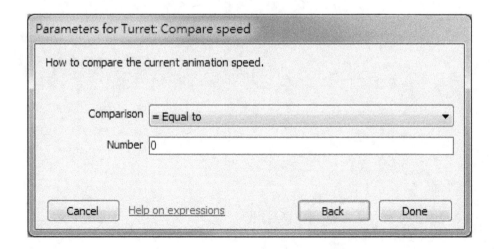

Then you define a logical comparison as needed:

Then you click Add action to pick an object for carrying about an action:

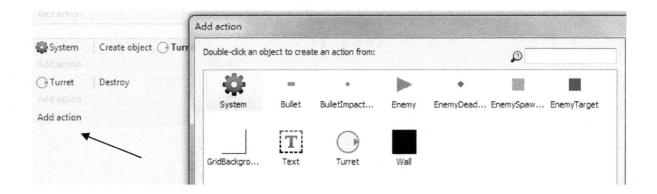

Then you pick the desired action and set the relevant value as needed, and add other actions if necessary:

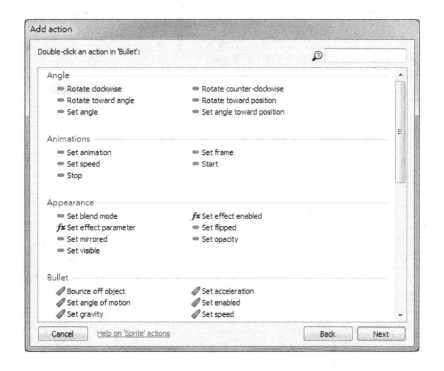

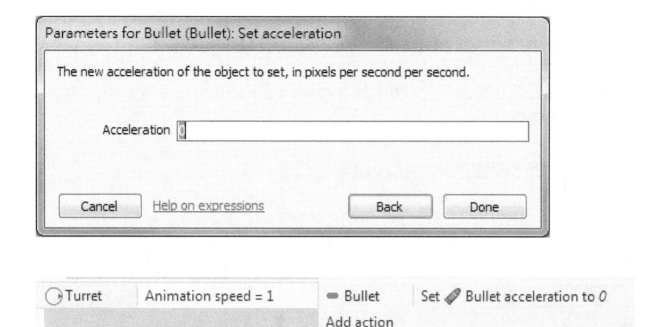

The resulting event sheet shows all the rules you have defined for the layout. Each layout can be associated with one event sheet:

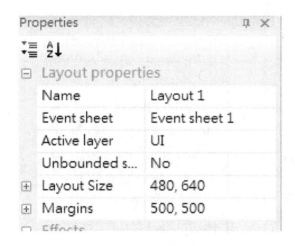

Can I write script and use it in CONSTRUCT/C2?

Yes. There is an action which allows you to invoke a script from within the game.

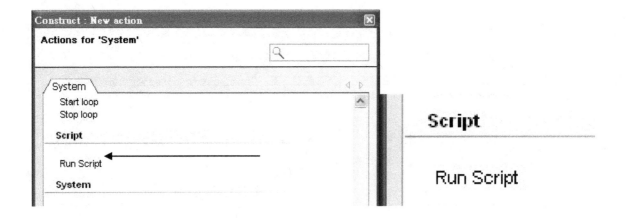

The script needs to be written in the Python language.

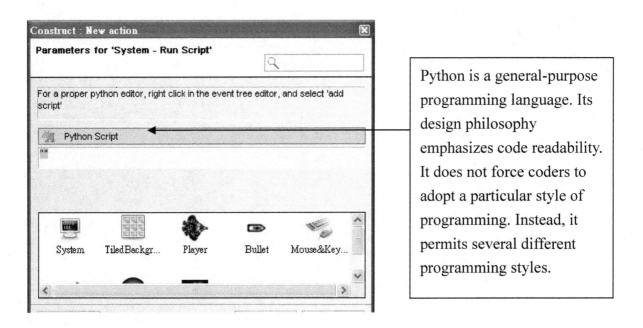

Python is a general-purpose programming language. Its design philosophy emphasizes code readability. It does not force coders to adopt a particular style of programming. Instead, it permits several different programming styles.

Note that you must explicitly turn on the scripting option. The python25.dll file must also be distributed together with your game file.

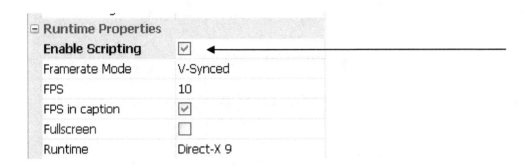

With C2, you are recommended to make use of the various actions of the System object as much as possible instead of writing scripts.

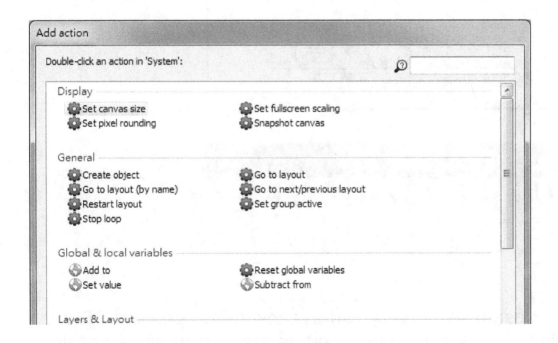

Separating graphic design from game design...

Through the CONSTRUCT/C2 picture editor you can import graphics for further processing. You can load an image into it, or simply copy and paste from another paint program.

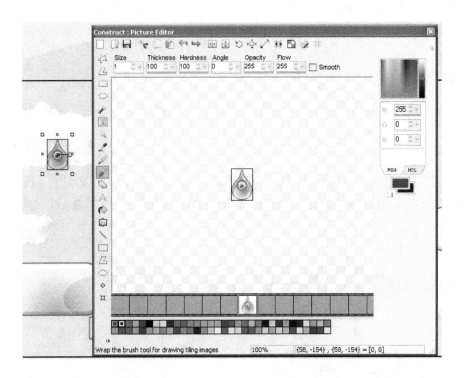

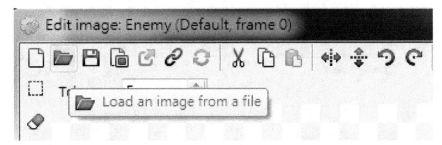

Graphic design is a very time consuming process. For an animation to look good you need as many frames as possible.

And you need to create animations for different situations in different directions. That means there are MANY frames to create.

Once you are into the graphic and animation work, the entire game creation process will slow down. A common problem is for the programming team to wait for finished artworks and animations from the media team prior to putting things together.

Assuming what you have got is a small team, I would suggest that you clearly break down the game creation process into two sub-processes, with one focusing on the logical "programming" side and another on media (graphics, animation, sound effects...etc) development.

During level design, the programming guy does not really have to use "real stuff". Object actions and events can be designed and implemented through using simple symbolic artworks. For example, instead of waiting for the media design guy to get you a finished Jet you can use a basic plane-like artwork for configuring all the relevant properties, events and actions first.

 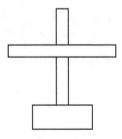

Once the programming works are done and fully tested you may slowly import and "fit in" the real stuff.

For your information, the graphic design guy would need to prepare and implement different animation sequences for the object. The actual use of these sequences is usually determined by the programming guy, through logics implemented in the event mechanisms.

As previously said, you can always prepare graphics via another paint program, then "export" to the CONSTRUCT picture editor through COPY and PASTE OR SAVE and OPEN:

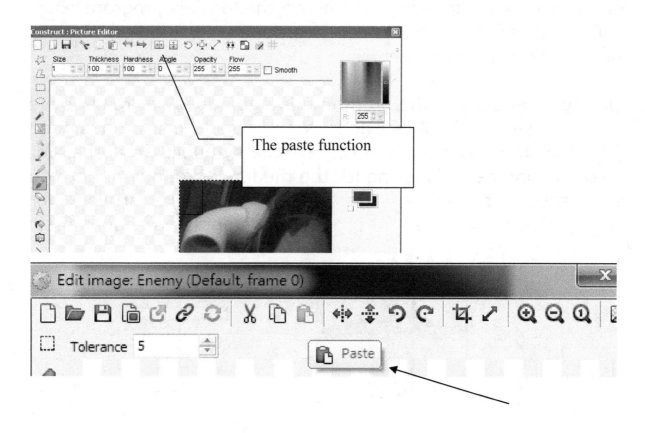

The paste function

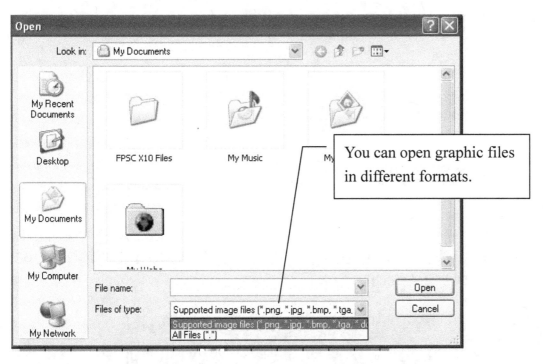

You can open graphic files in different formats.

The C2 picture editor is highly similar:

Very importantly, you can fine tune the collision polygon of an object via the picture editor in C2:

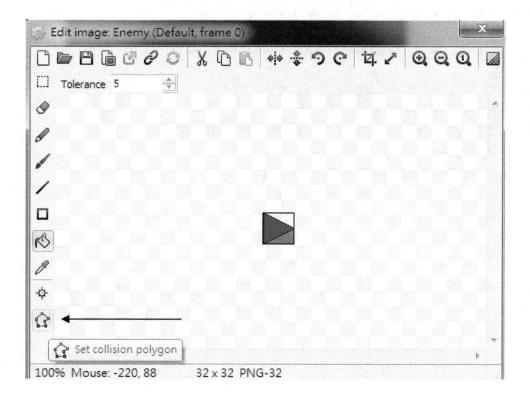

You ca right click on an image to call up this menu:

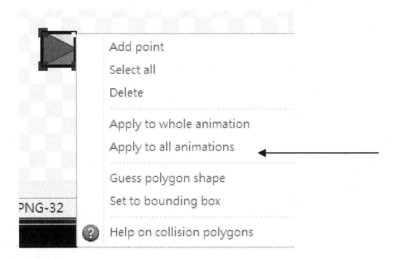

By default there is already a collision polygon "guessed" by the program so you do not need to make a custom one, UNLESS the default one is not up to your satisfaction. Also note that background tile does not use collision polygon at all.

By default the collision polygons are not shown. However, you can choose to display them.

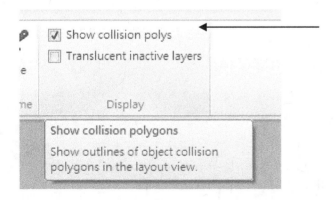

I am confused – how do the terms Application, Game,

Layout, and Window relate to each others?

In the context of CONSTRUCT game creation:

- an application represents a game
- a layout holds a game level
- an application shows up on your desktop through its window
- each application should have only one window (for purpose of game display)
- each application can have one or more layouts

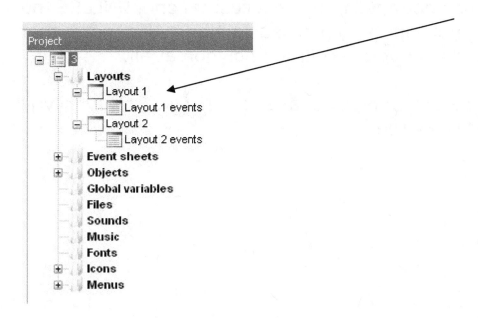

- each layout can belong to only one application
- a CAP file is a unit for saving works in CONSTRUCT
- each CAP file holds one and only one application

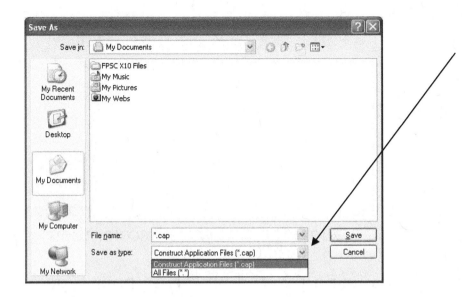

When you create a new program in CONSTRUCT, you can choose to create an application or a DirectX game.

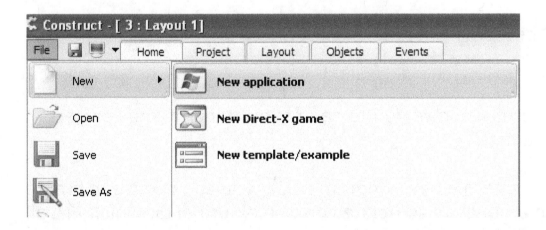

A game is just a specialty type of application, with different display characteristics. A modern game is expected to make use of DirectX. You can actually change the runtime display type via the application properties:

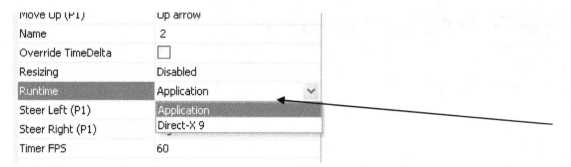

There is nothing to stop you from creating a "game-like application" that runs without DirectX. However, performance will likely suffer (DirectX can allow for hardware acceleration).

If you are creating games using C2, the preferred built type is HTML5. DirectX is no longer emphasized since it is not available on non-Windows platforms. Also, the C2 file format is .capx:

Construct 2 compressed project (*.capx)

This file format allows you to save everything of your project in one single file.

When you create a new program in C2, you can choose to create based on a bunch of templates and blank projects, which are all configured with some specific properties.

Select template or example

Select a template to start with or an example to open:

New empty project
Create a new empty project with default settings.

New retro style project
Create a platform-neutral project with settings and objects suited to retro style games (such as pixellated rather than smooth scaling).

New empty SD landscape 4:3 project
Create a new empty project with a standard definition 4:3 landscape screen.

New empty SD portrait 4:3 project
Create a new empty project with a standard definition 4:3 portrait screen.

New empty SD landscape 16:9 project
Create a new empty project with a standard definition 16:9 landscape screen.

New empty SD portrait 16:9 project
Create a new empty project with a standard definition 16:9 portrait screen.

New empty HD landscape 720p project

Help   Open   Cancel

If you want your project to be platform neutral, you may want to create a retro style project, which is a category that represents pixellated games full of chunky 2D style pixel arts.

What is the relationship between a window, a layout and a layer?

On a Windows desktop, all applications exist in the form of a "window". A window displays a layout. A layout contains a game level. You may think of a window as a view port for viewing a layout (and the game level presented by the layout).

Each layout can have multiple layers. Layers is a design time feature which allows you to easily arrange the level objects. Put it this way, a flat layout means there is only one layer. When multiple layers are involved, you need to determine how your objects are to be placed (for example, all background objects at one layer and other active objects on another layer).

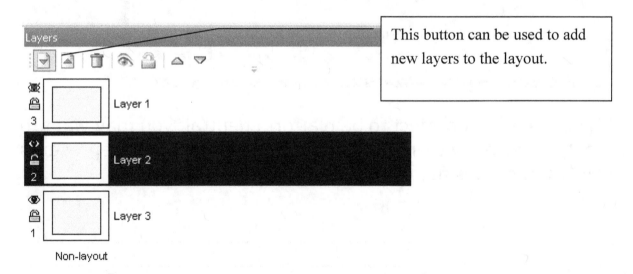

This button can be used to add new layers to the layout.

Visually, a window can be made as large as or larger than a layout. A layout, however, can never go "outside" of a window during display. Window size properties are set as application properties:

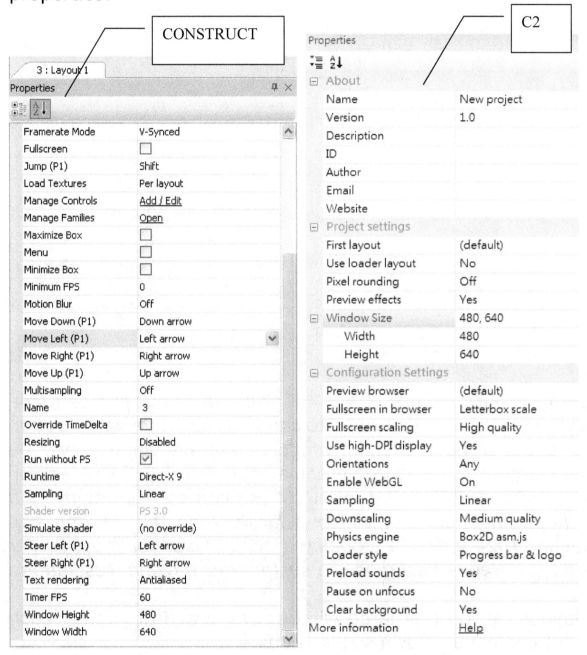

In C2, you can add multiple layers to a layout as well. However, only one can be made active at a time (all newly inserted objects are placed on the active layer by default).

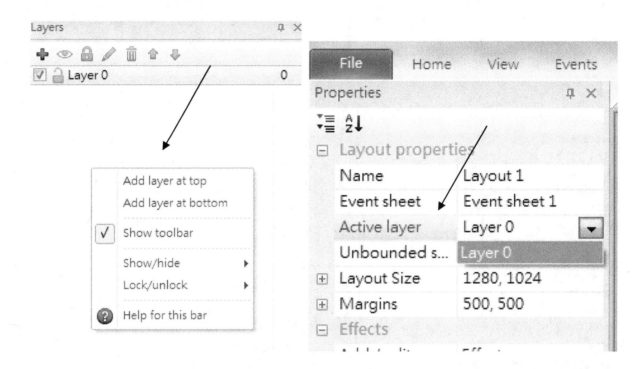

Talking about the "actual size" in pixels, a layout can be made way larger than a window (scrolling allows one to walk through the layout through a small window). A window can never be made larger than the max viewable area of the Windows desktop (say, 1600 x 1200 on a typical 20" monitor configuration). *You do not want a window which is larger than the desktop size though. 1024 x 768 is probably a good choice for most earlier desktops. Newer desktops can sustain much higher resolution.*

A layout can go real large without any practical limits! Each layout can have its own size settings.

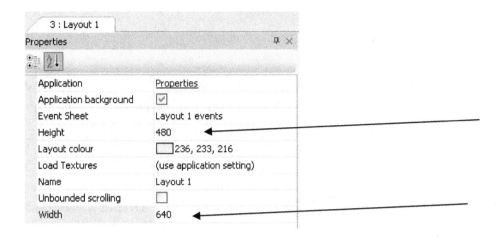

Because the layers are "merged" for display at runtime, end users won't be able to tell the existence of multiple layers on a layout.

Layers are ideal for organizing objects. You can selectively make some layers invisible:

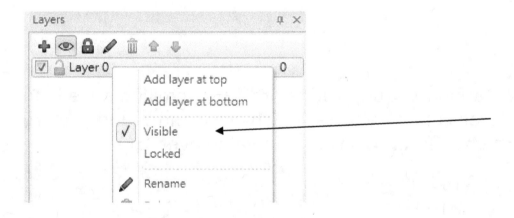

Do note that a layout has an event sheet. A layer does not.

Multiple layers and screen effects

Having multiple layers is good if you want to set fancy background scrolling effects. Both CONSTRUCT and C2 support this. Each layer can have its own scrolling speed, and some layers can even be made stationary.

Settings on layer scrolling are made on a per layer basis, via the Parallax option.

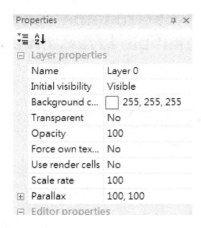

0, 0 means stationary. 100, 100 is ordinary scrolling speed. To be precise, Parallax has 2 values, which are X and Y, and you are free to set them differently, even to a value over 100.

Windows settings

To ensure nothing stupid can happen when your game is run, I don't think you should give your user too much freedom in manipulating the display window. Corresponding restrictions can be configured via the various application properties (note: running the game full screen is usually recommended):

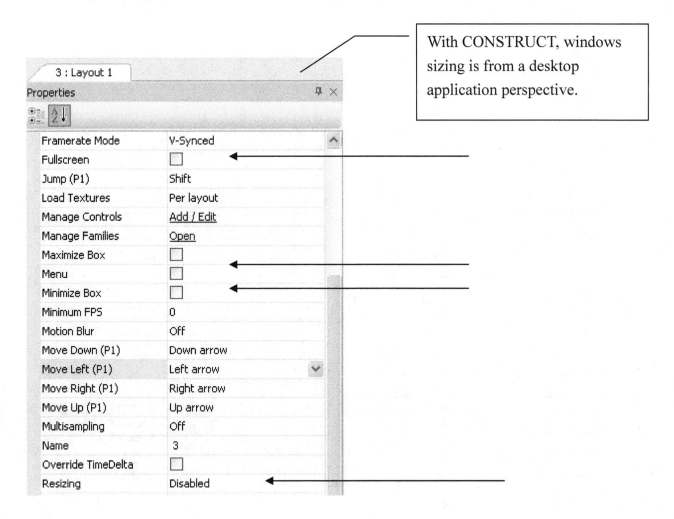

With CONSTRUCT, windows sizing is from a desktop application perspective.

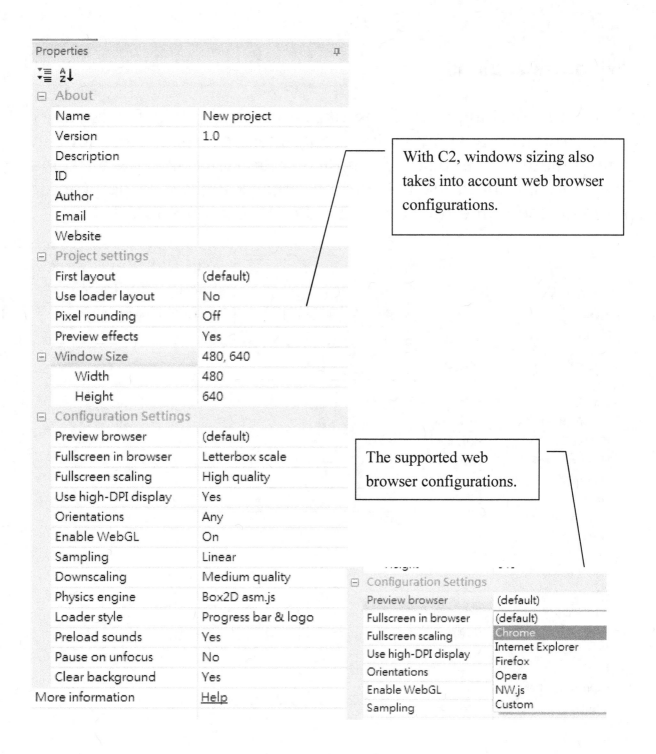

Properties

About
Name	New project
Version	1.0
Description	
ID	
Author	
Email	
Website	

Project settings
First layout	(default)
Use loader layout	No
Pixel rounding	Off
Preview effects	Yes

Window Size — 480, 640
| Width | 480 |
| Height | 640 |

Configuration Settings
Preview browser	(default)
Fullscreen in browser	Letterbox scale
Fullscreen scaling	High quality
Use high-DPI display	Yes
Orientations	Any
Enable WebGL	On
Sampling	Linear
Downscaling	Medium quality
Physics engine	Box2D asm.js
Loader style	Progress bar & logo
Preload sounds	Yes
Pause on unfocus	No
Clear background	Yes

More information — Help

With C2, windows sizing also takes into account web browser configurations.

The supported web browser configurations.

Configuration Settings
Preview browser	(default)
Fullscreen in browser	(default)
Fullscreen scaling	Chrome
Use high-DPI display	Internet Explorer
	Firefox
Orientations	Opera
Enable WebGL	NW.js
Sampling	Custom

What is the relationship between a layout and an Event

Sheet?

The Event Sheet is where you start adding new events to the layout. **This is true for both CONSTRUCT and C2.**

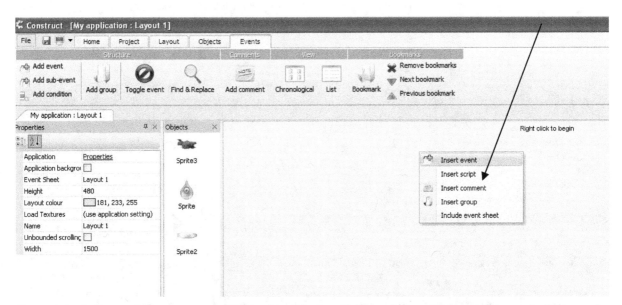

Put it this way, an event sheet is linked to the current layout. Generally you are given one and only one event sheet per layout.

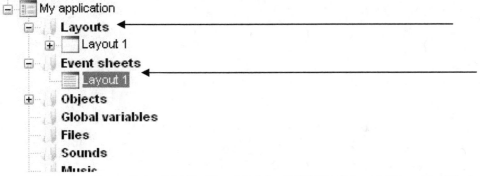

The display of events is done as a list, with entries listed one after another. You can choose between two different ways of displaying the events.

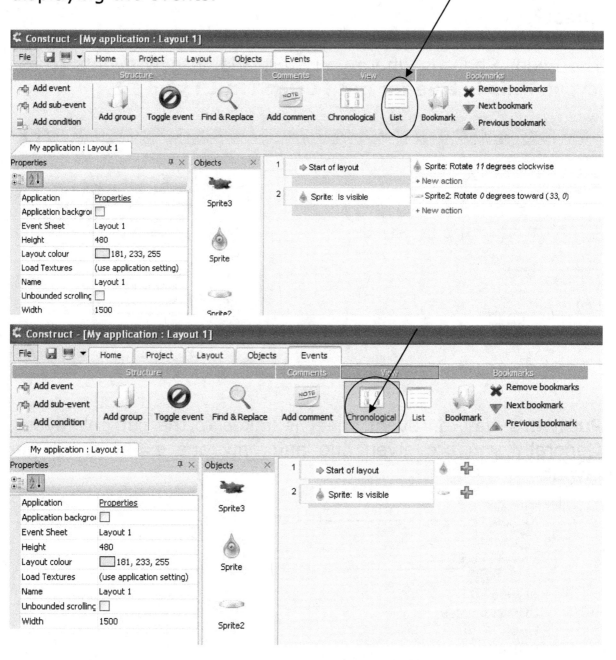

On the event sheet you can right click on an event entry and perform copy & paste of event entries.

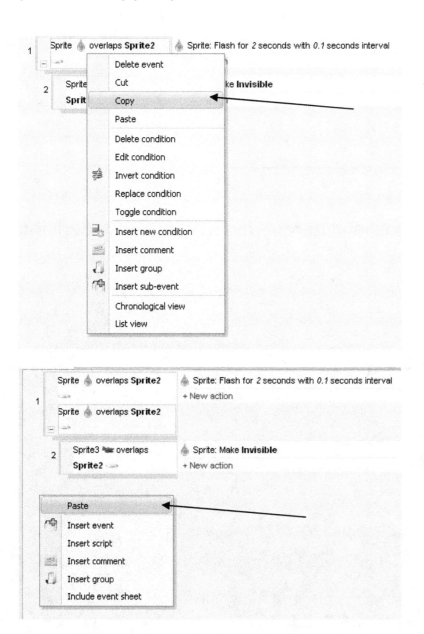

You can also create INVERTED condition (i.e. a NOT condition) by inverting an existing condition.

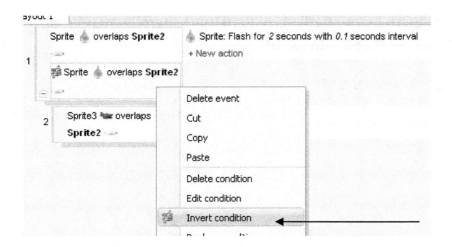

The C2 event sheet has a different look, but the underlying concepts are the same:

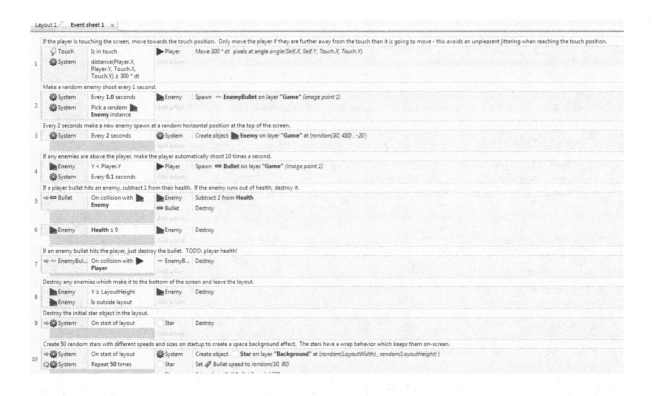

Why should I optimize the event list?

The CONSTRUCT/C2 engine will read through an event list at regular time intervals. The more entries you have in the list, the slower your game is going to run since the program will need to spend longer time in scanning the list.

You should go over the event list from within the Event Sheet. Just read the entries one by one, see if any of them is actually irrelevant or meaningless (no real effects), and make deletion or replacement as necessary. *Programmers in the programming world do this kind of code walk through all the time.*

Pay attention to any loop that shows up in the list. Things improperly done inside a loop can drag down performance big time (since the improper action is kept repeating over and over again)!

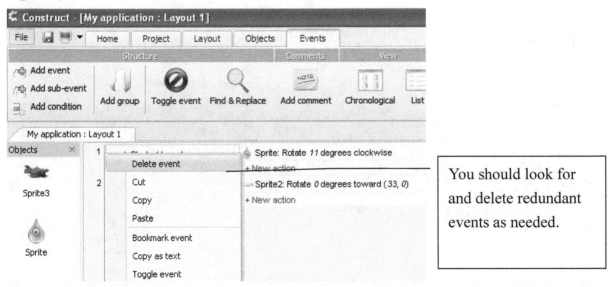

You should look for and delete redundant events as needed.

An EXAMPLE: this event has a problem:

Sprite overlaps **Sprite2** Sprite3: Rotate *44* degrees clockwise

+ New action

It says as long as the two sprites are not overlapping, sprite 3 will rotate 44 degrees.

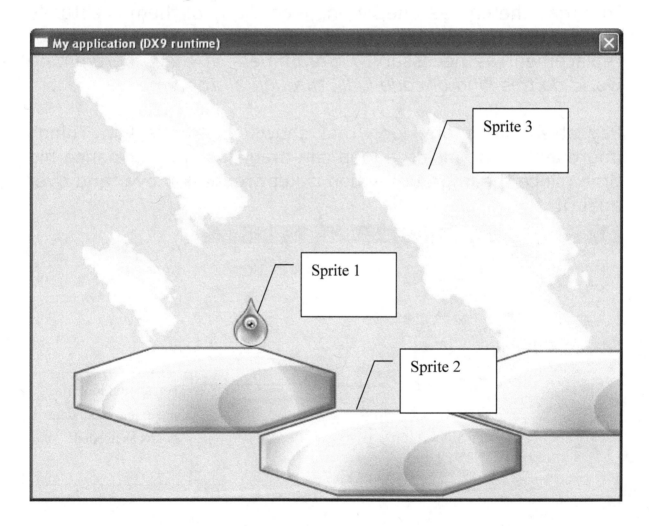

Because sprite 1 will never overlap with sprite 2 (sprite 2 is a platform), sprite 3 will keep rotating non-stop.

This one also has a problem:

Both conditions belong to the same event entry, and they are contradicting with one another. In other words, this event will never occur.

Implementing IF THEN ELSE in the Event Sheet

An IF THEN ELSE kind of logic is best to be created on the Event Sheet. Note that CONSTRUCT DOES NOT have true IF THEN ELSE construct. We are just trying to simulate one.

Refer to the examples below:

This one is pretty straightforward – if they overlap, sprite 1 will flash.

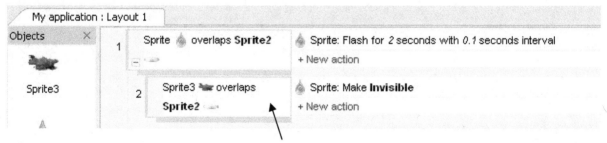

This time we have a sub-event as the second entry, saying if sprite 2 overlaps with sprite 3 then sprite 1 will disappear. Do note that this sub-event will be evaluated only if the first event it belongs to is evaluated to true. Technically this is NOT an IF THEN ELSE.

To simulate an ELSE logic (CONSTRUCT does not have a true

ELSE operator), simply setup a second condition which has the same condition and then have it INVERTED. When the evaluation process flows through these entries, an effect of ELSE will naturally take place.

In C2, the logic works the same but the display is different. When you add a condition it will provide a dialog box that guides you through setting up the logic.

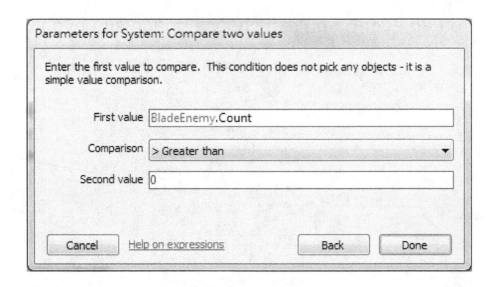

A number of comparison operations are possible.

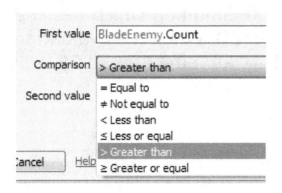

When multiple conditions are specified on the same line, they form an AND relationships - all conditions need to be matched.

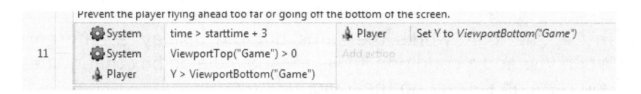

If you right click on an event, you can choose to add sub event:

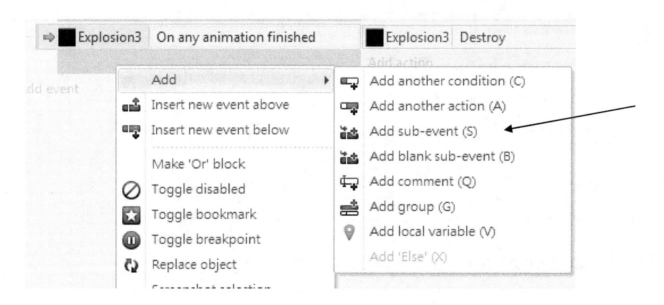

A blank sub event is a place holder which allows you to define the details later.

If you want to make an OR relationship, first choose Make OR block before adding another condition:

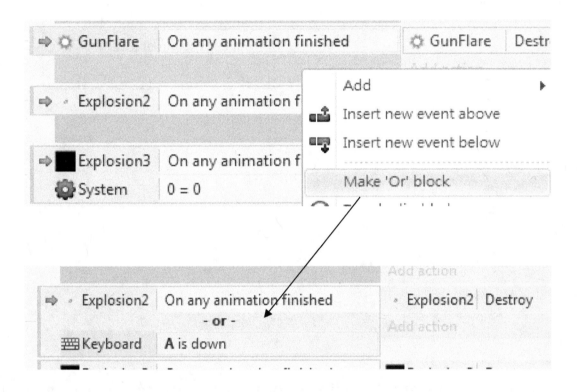

Cloning VS Copying: What is the difference?

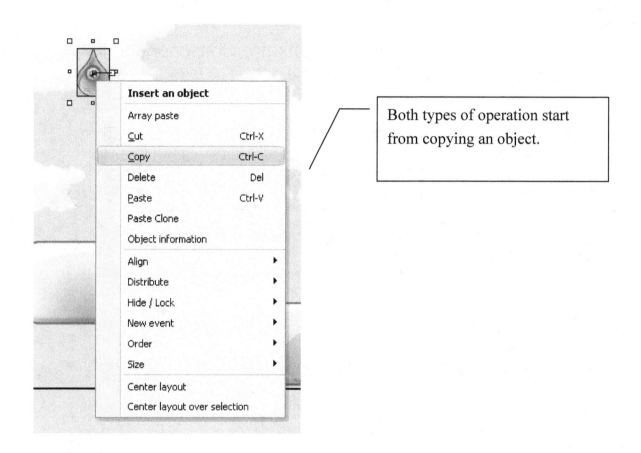

Both types of operation start from copying an object.

Cloning an object means creating a new separated object out of an existing object. Copying/duplicating an object means creating new occurrence(s) of it. Both functions can be accessed when you right click on a sprite.

Copy and Paste = copying/making a duplicate (i.e. a pasted object).
Copy and Paste Clone = cloning.

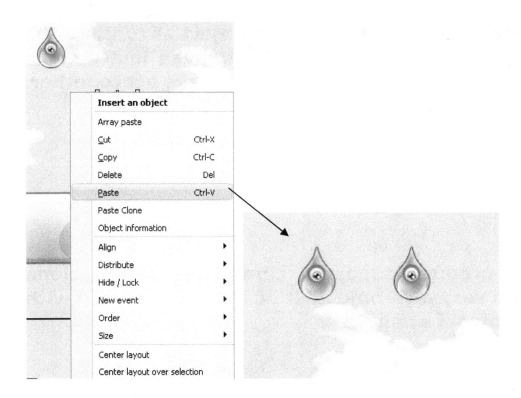

If you modify the look and properties of a pasted object, you are in fact modifying the original source object.

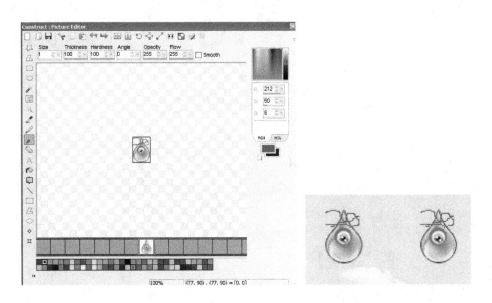

In fact, when you move the source object at runtime the pasted object will also move following the instructions given to the source object. They will always act together.

When you produce a pasted clone, the pasted clone becomes its very own object. It has no relationship with the source object at all.

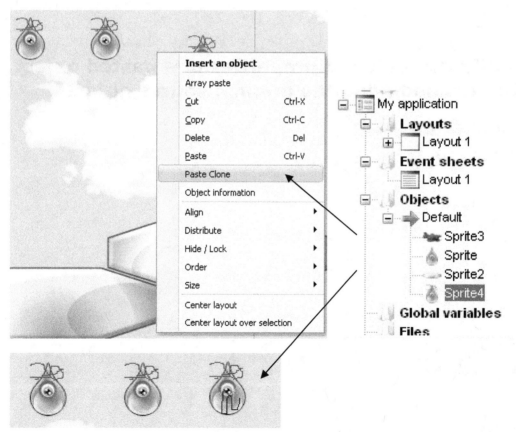

Copyright 2015. **The HobbyPRESS (Hong Kong)**. All rights reserved.

One easy way to tell whether an object is a duplicate or a clone -> just check the application properties and see if the object has its own sprite entry. With its own sprite entry, it means it is a totally independent object.

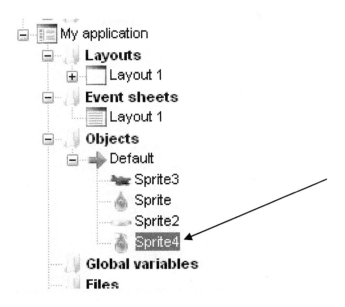

In C2, when you right click an object you can choose to clone object type. The new object is one totally independent of the original. If, however, you choose to copy and paste, the new one produced is a duplicate.

Do NOT judge based on the object UID. Even a duplicate will have its own UID.

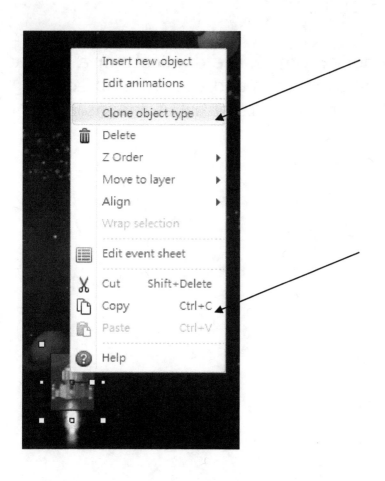

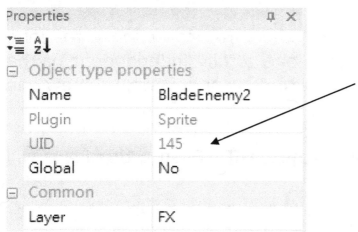

Effects on duplicated/pasted objects

When an object has, say, 4 duplicates made on the same layout, there is always only ONE shown in the event sheet. In other words, you cannot manipulate each individual duplicate programmatically by default.

Let's refer to this simple example. I want to specify that whenever sprite collides with sprite 4, sprite 3 will flash. From the event wizard there is no way I can specify WHICH sprite (remember I have a duplicated sprite created?) to use in defining the condition and the action.

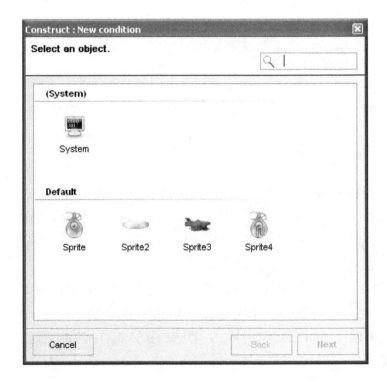

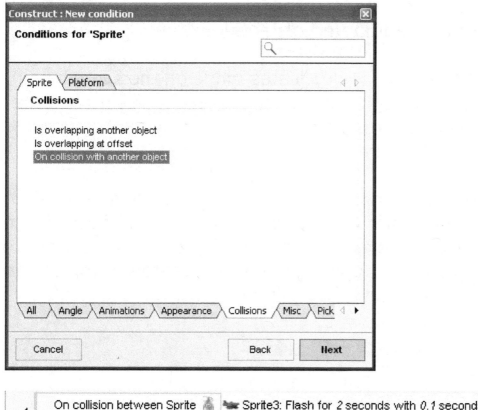

The event condition is that whenever collision takes place between sprite and sprite 4 (you cannot specify a particular duplicate of sprite anyway), sprite 3 will flash.

The resulting runtime behavior of this setup is that when either the source sprite or the pasted sprite collides with sprite 4, the event condition is met and flashing takes place immediately. This holds true for both CONSTRUCT and C2.

Object Instance Variables

In C2 an object can have its own instance variable. You can always add instance variables of type number, boolean or text to an object:

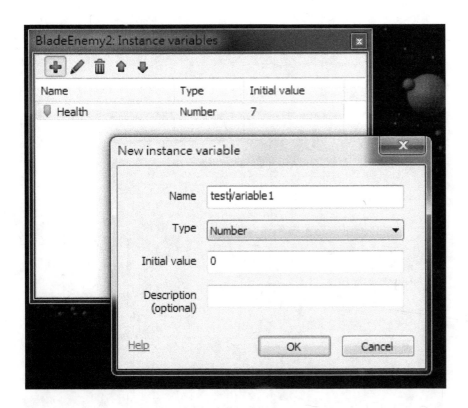

These variables can be manipulated via Event conditions and actions:

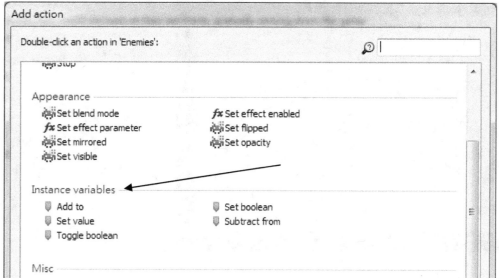

You may use instance variable to implement, say, the health of an object:

Object Families

In C2 you may use Families to group objects together. You cannot mix and match different object types in the same family though. You may right click on Families and choose Add Family:

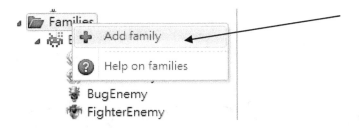

With this feature, it would be much easier to define events that affect the entire family. However, the Free edition of C2 does not support this.

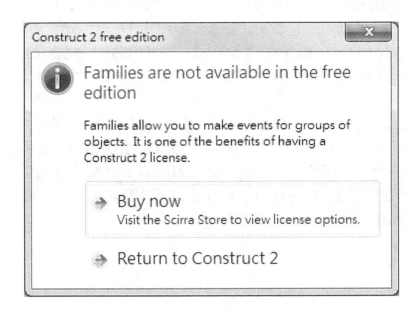

Development Tools Configuration

What configuration should I use for my CONSTRUCT/C2

development station?

A development station for CONSTRUCT/C2 does not have to be real fast and powerful. I think a reasonable configuration for elementary level game creation in the modern days would entail, at the least, a P4 dual core processor, 3GB+ RAMs, 160GB+ hard disk ...etc. I always recommend that you have at least TWO hard disks installed on the same computer, with Norton GHOST (a disk cloning program) in place to create a complete image of your primary disk so if something goes wrong you can recover the development settings quickly by restoring from the image.

Working data backup is different – you need to regularly backup your working data into at least TWO different places, such as a high capacity SD card and a USB connected external hard disk. SCSI, IDE, SATA... all these don't really matter. CONSTRUCT will not run better just because it is on a SCSI disk.

What is the recommended disk layout for my CONSTRUCT

/C2 development station?

Personally I would suggest that you maintain the following partitions:

- a partition for the Windows OS
- a partition for CONSTRUCT/C2 and all other development tools
- a partition for all the working data (game graphics, the game application files, sound effect files ...etc)

If you have a second hard disk, on this second disk you should have:

- a partition for Norton Ghost to build and keep clone images
- a partition for making backups of the working data
- a partition for Windows virtual memory (i.e. disk swapping)
- a partition for special purpose swapping (when you use heavy duty graphic processing application like Photoshop then you will need this for sure)

Note that the C2 installation is portable so in theory you can even run it on a USB disk!

How much disk space should I keep for CONSTRUCT?

Full installation takes approximately 60MB.

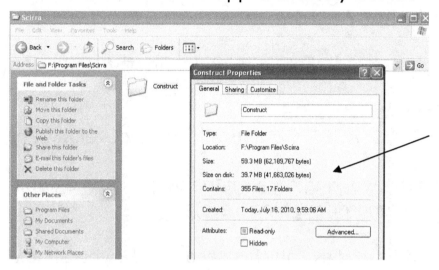

By default, the CONSTRUCT program has the following folder structure:

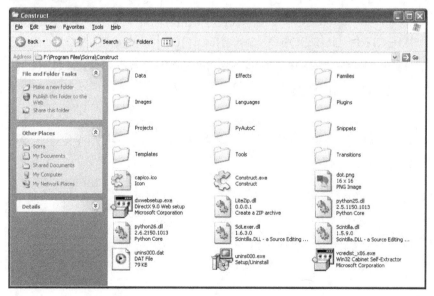

Because you may want to install additional plugins at a later time, I would say you better keep several hundred MBs of free space for everything CONSTRUCT related.

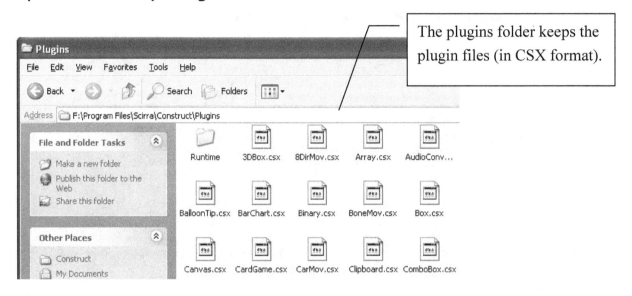

The plugins folder keeps the plugin files (in CSX format).

A list of plugins can be found here: http://sourceforge.net/apps/mediawiki/construct/index.php?title=Object_List

From within your game, it is possible to find out the plugins that are in use, by right clicking on the application.

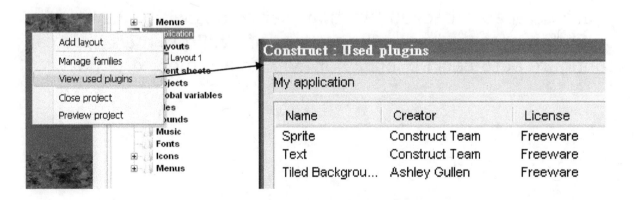

Copyright 2015. **The HobbyPRESS (Hong Kong)**. All rights reserved.

How much disk space should I keep for C2?

Full installation takes approximately 380MB.

There is an auto backup function that comes with C2. You click on Preferences to change the settings of C2. From there, you can configure auto backup locally or even to a remote dropbox.

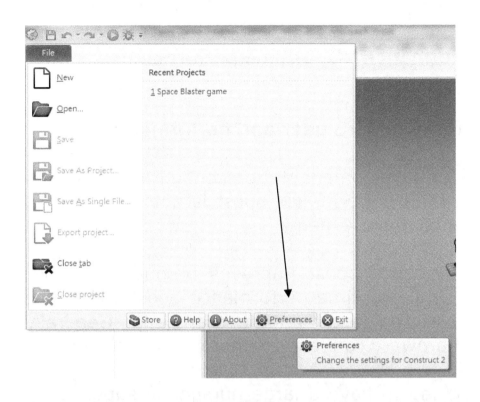

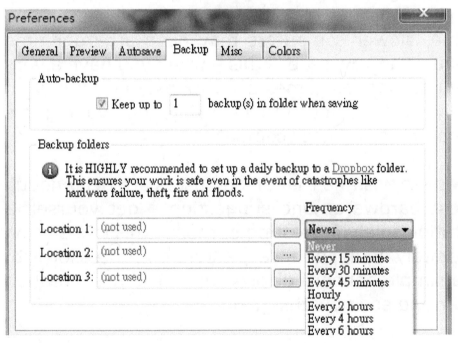

Design time performance VS runtime performance

Design-end performance VS user-end performance

When you plan your development station configuration, keep in mind that design time performance boost is not the same as runtime performance improvement.

Design time performance boost improves productivity (your tools run faster), while runtime performance boost allows the game you create to run faster on the client end. Generally speaking, better hardware can lead to improvement on both.

If your game is going to have a large number of super fancy graphics and animations plus tons of rich objects all showing up at the same time, slower computers may have a harder time working things out. The key issue is this – when you have a very fast development station, all games can run fast in front of you. This can actually mislead you into believing that your game could run as smooth on the user computers.

It may not be wise to assume that all end users are rich enough to own the latest hardware. One suggestion – get yourself a separate test station solely for testing purpose. This test station should be moderately equipped – say, a Celeron processor with 1GB RAM and a simple onboard display unit. Test your creation on this computer and see how things go.

What amount of memory should I install in my development station? Do I need a dual core processor?

Along the process of game creation you often need to keep multiple applications (graphics, effects, game...etc) running at the same time, therefore the more RAM you have the better (and RAM is dirt cheap these days anyway).

CONSTRUCT is a 32bit based platform. However, it can run on 32bit/64bit based Windows. If you run it under 64bit Windows 7 you should run it under the Windows 7 Compatible mode. The maximum amount of memory that can be utilized by a 32bit Windows is roughly 3.3GB. Therefore, practically speaking a 3GB configuration would be all that you need. Most modern motherboards can let you install 3GBs or more of RAM (2GB + 1GB or 1GB + 1GB + 1GB).

CONSTRUCT itself was NOT written to take advantage of multiple processor cores. Therefore, if you are running only CONSTRUCT and nothing else then there would be no performance gain by using dual core processor. HOWEVER, as said before along the process of game creation you will very likely need to keep multiple applications running at the same time. Therefore, you may find a dual core processor beneficial.

In fact you can monitor CPU utilization via the Windows Task Manager. You can press CTRL ALT DEL to activate it.

Do this when CONSTRUCT is running. If you see constantly high utilization here (80% or higher), a processor upgrade may become necessary. If you see heavy page file usage from the line chart, that means disk swapping is frequent – you don't have sufficient RAM in the system.

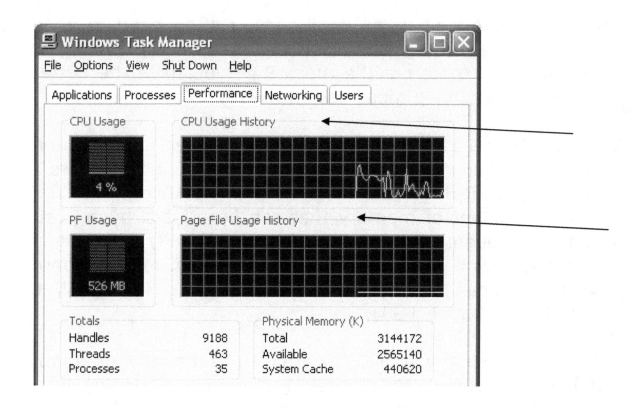

C2 can go both 32 bit and 64 bit - if you are using 64 bit Windows then the 64 bit version will be installed. It is not power hungry but RAM is cheap so having more wouldn't hurt for sure. ^4 bit Windows can accommodate way more RAM anyway.

How do I optimize on my development station?

First of all you need to identify the processes that belong to CONSTRUCT. You can do this via the Windows Task Manager.

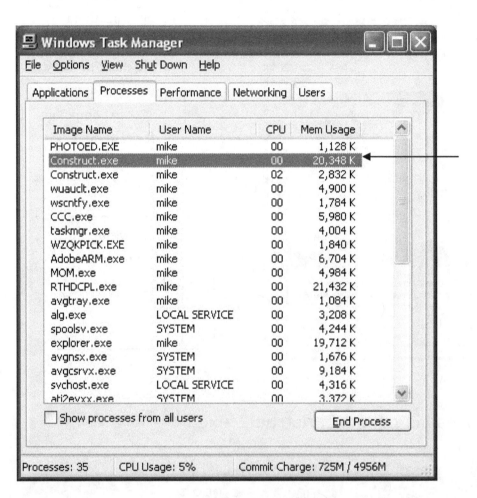

You can right click on the relevant processes and set the proper priority. By default the priority level is Normal. You may try to set it to High. *A "High" value here should not lead to system instability.*

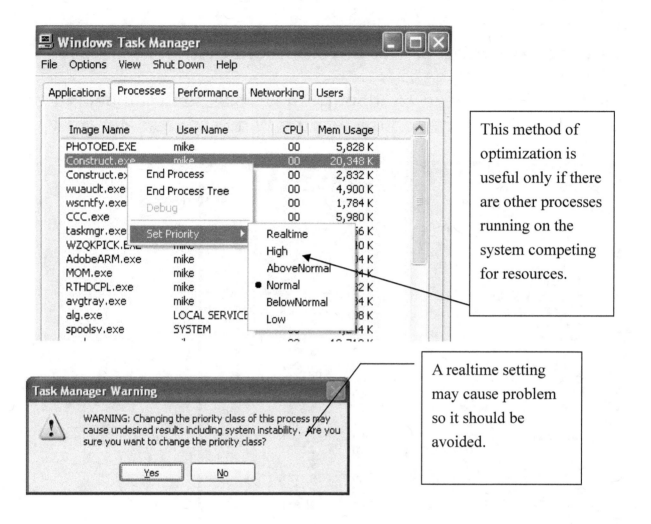

This method of optimization is useful only if there are other processes running on the system competing for resources.

A realtime setting may cause problem so it should be avoided.

For C2, the process is called Construct2.exe.

Image Name	User Name	CPU	Mem Usage
CCC.exe	user	00	10,152 K
conhost.exe	user	00	288 K
Construct2.exe	user	00	76,460 K
csrss.exe		00	1,416 K

Do I need a high performance graphic card in my

CONSTRUCT development station?

Generally speaking, onboard integrated graphic display is slower than a dedicated display card. This holds true for ALL windows applications. CONSTRUCT is not demanding in terms of graphic display power. With hardware acceleration certain display cards may render improved performance at runtime though. The thing is, design time performance improvement on your desk may not translate into run time performance gain on the user end. What if your target users do not have the kind of highly powerful display card that you have?

My recommendation is that so long as hardware acceleration is not involved, any modern graphic display unit will do. I personally prefer dedicated display cards more simply because they have their very own onboard RAM (at least 64MB - 128MB/256MB recommended) so the main system memory can be conserved (no need to share memory with the display). **When hardware acceleration is desired, DirectX support must be implemented.** Higher end display cards using ATI/NVIDIA chips are quite affordable these days. Most of them can support DirectX 9 or above without any problems.

C2 always checks for the status of your display card driver and makes recommendation accordingly. It is a very nice feature to have!

Do I need a large chunk of Video RAM on my graphic card?

How do I keep track of the amount of available Video RAM?

CONSTRUCT does not specifically ask for a particular amount of Video RAM, although "64MB is recommended". If you want your production environment to be of rich color (such as 32 bit color depth) and high resolution than of course you will need more. Modern display cards usually come with 1GB of video RAM anyway.

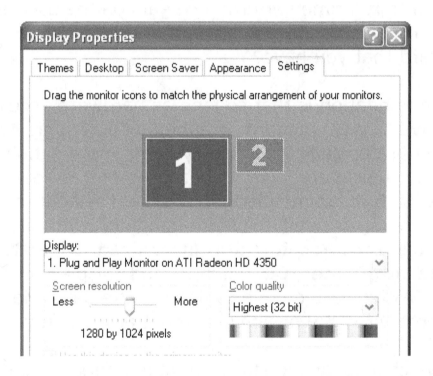

Our recommendation: set aside at least 128MB of video memory if you are using an integrated chipset. 256MB preferred. This can be done from the BIOS. See if it helps. If not, install the latest display driver and also the DirectX driver and retry. Some older SIS chipsets can let you allocate 64MB at the max, which may not be sufficient at all.

Runtime configuration is not easy to control. Different computers have different configuration and there is no way for you to predetermine the available video memory.

Rich textures consume video memory. A conservative way to deal with video memory usage would be to load textures on a per layout basis instead of loading all textures at application start. This can be done by specifying the runtime properties:

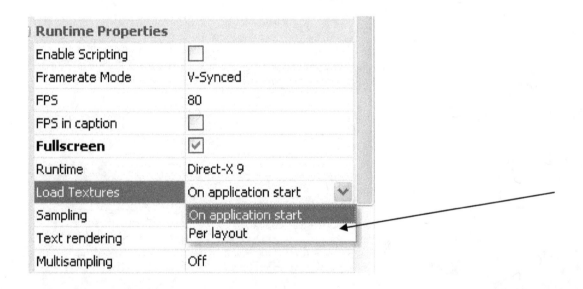

To keep track of video memory usage at runtime, you need to uncheck the full screen option:

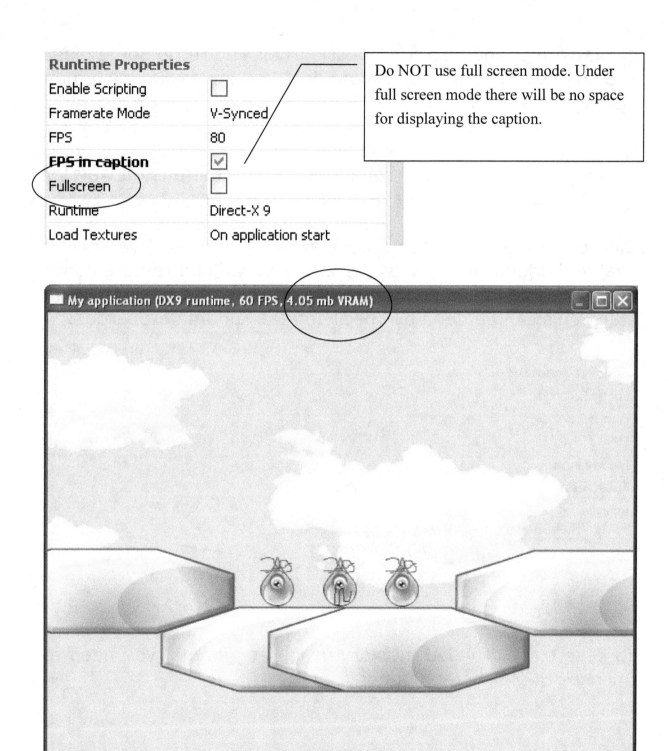

Runtime Properties

Enable Scripting	☐
Framerate Mode	V-Synced
FPS	80
FPS in caption	☑
Fullscreen	☐
Runtime	Direct-X 9
Load Textures	On application start

Do NOT use full screen mode. Under full screen mode there will be no space for displaying the caption.

My application (DX9 runtime, 60 FPS, 4.05 mb VRAM)

In C2, there are configuration settings that are video performance related. For example, if you use high quality full screen scaling you will need a higher capacity video card for sure.

High DPI display can also incur a performance tradeoff:

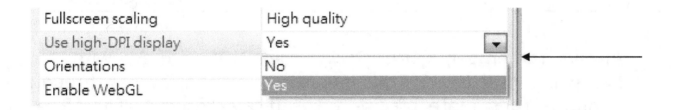

Do I need DirectX 9 or DirectX 10 installed?

In fact, at the time you install CONSTRUCT, the installation routine will prompt you to install DirectX. DirectX9 is sufficient, although it would not hurt to have a later version. If you are using Windows 7 or later, chance is that you are having a version which is pretty updated.

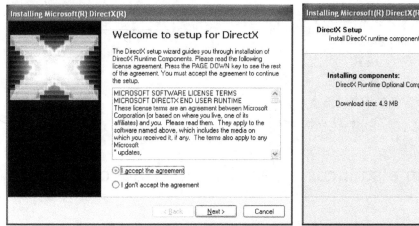 

Always remember, CONSTRUCT does NOT interact with the hardware directly. It manipulates your hardware through Windows (and more precise – the display driver). Therefore, hardware is more or less a Windows driver issue rather than a CONSTRUCT specific issue.

You should always opt for Windows Certified Drivers. If you are using a high end display solution such as a NVIDIA display card, there are many settings you can fine tune. It would not hurt to try them out.

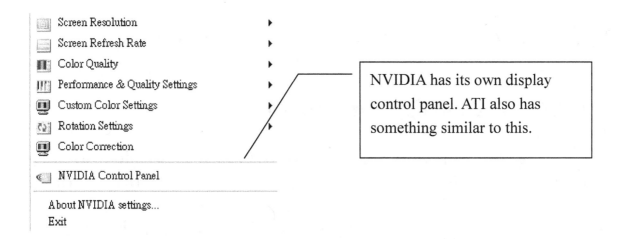

Screen Resolution ▶
Screen Refresh Rate ▶
Color Quality ▶
Performance & Quality Settings ▶
Custom Color Settings ▶
Rotation Settings ▶
Color Correction

NVIDIA Control Panel

About NVIDIA settings...
Exit

NVIDIA has its own display control panel. ATI also has something similar to this.

If the display driver is corrupted or the DirectX version in use is outdated, you may receive this kind of error when trying to preview the layout:

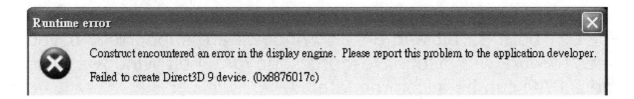

Runtime error ☒

❌ Construct encountered an error in the display engine. Please report this problem to the application developer.

Failed to create Direct3D 9 device. (0x8876017c)

Which Windows version should be used to power my

CONSTRUCT development station?

My personal recommendation is Windows 7. It is stable and very reliable. Vista itself is way too power hungry. It eats up half of all system resources even when not running anything. Windows Server 2003/2008 are never optimized for front end applications. Windows 8 is too new and I just don't like its Metro interface.

For CONSTRUCT: you should use a 32-bit Windows. If you use a 64-bit Windows to run CONSTRUCT, run it under the Compatible Mode.

For C2: both 32 bit and 64 bit Windows are supported. If you need to work with a lot of resources, go for 64 bit Windows since more RAM can be accommodated.

Do NOT use Windows 8. It is not really good for development use.

What other development tools should I install on my computer?

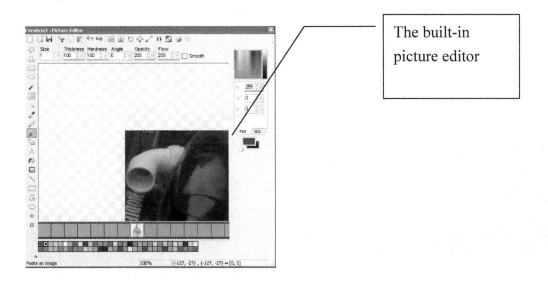

The built-in picture editor

CONSTRUCT's graphic editor is a pretty basic one. To create very fancy graphics you'll need something more powerful. The Paint.NET software by dotPDN LLC is free and is very powerful so I would not hesitate to recommend it.

First you create and save your graphics with a third party tool, then you get them imported into CONSTRUCT for further editing and customization. Popular formats like TGA, BMP, JPG and PNG are all supported.

You also need a good virus scanner for proper virus protection. AVG is free is and is pretty reliable.

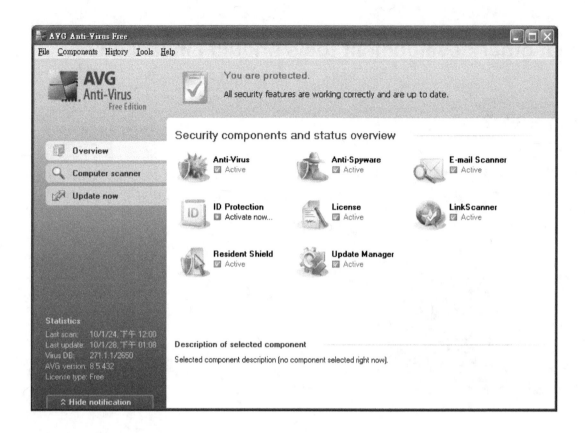

As of the time of this writing, to the best of my knowledge there is no specific virus attack targeting the CONSTRUCT application files (in CAP format). There is also no specific virus attack targeting the C2 compressed application files (in CAPX format).

Still, for your peace of mind it is best to have a proper anti-virus solution in place.

What tool can I use to open texture files of another format and

convert them to BMPs for further manipulation?

You need a conversion tool. One such tool is the LS Image Converter from Linos Software:

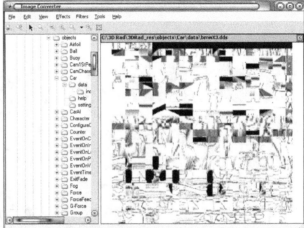

The Image Converter currently supports these image types:
IMPORT - PDF, PSD, PS, EPS, WBMP, WMF, EMF, PIC, JP2, JLS, FPX, RAW, DCM, CUT, IFF, DDS, PBM, PGM, PPM, RAF, RAS, XMB, XPB
EXPORT - BMP, JPEG, GIF, TIF, PNG, PCX, ICO, TGA, PSD, PS, EMF, JP2, FPX, RAW, PBM, PGM, PPM, XPB.

Smoothdraw is a paint program that can read files in a wide range of formats for further editing.

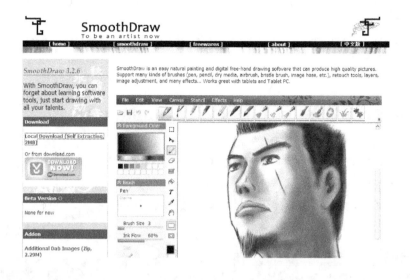

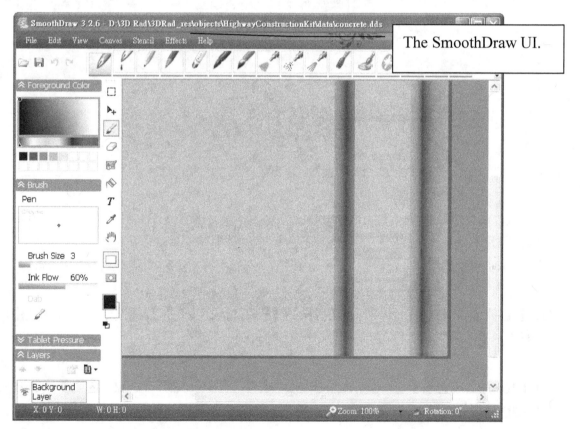

The SmoothDraw UI.

If you are making texture for wall tiles you should make them in multiples of 64, 128, or 256 pixels in size. Also, there is nothing to stop you from using higher color depth but at runtime performance issues may arise. For the sake of performance optimization you may want your BMP files to be saved in 256 Indexed Color Mode.

As of the time of this writing the latest version is version 4.

http://www.smoothdraw.com

If my hard drive crashes, what special procedures are necessary so I can reinstall CONSTRUCT onto a new drive?

What about C2?

You may reinstall CONSTRUCT from the downloaded file at any time. No special procedure of any sort is necessary.

You should not run CONSTRUCT without an active network connection. The installer is going to check for updates during installation. There are many useful plugins that may have to be separately downloaded as well (they don't come with the main installer file).

C2 is portable so you can simply backup the entire program folder and use it when the original folder is corrupted. Anytime you need to run the program simply click on construct2.exe.

Performance Concerns

What is the optimal display resolution and color depth for

CONSTRUCT/C2 to operate at design time?

Any resolution you feel comfort to work with. The higher the resolution the more workload your display card would have to handle. Most modern display cards, however, will do just fine at 1024 x 768 OR 1280 x 1024. In terms of color depth, you may simply stay with what you already have in your Windows OS. Due to advance in hardware performance, displaying large number of colors should not really slow things down in your production environment.

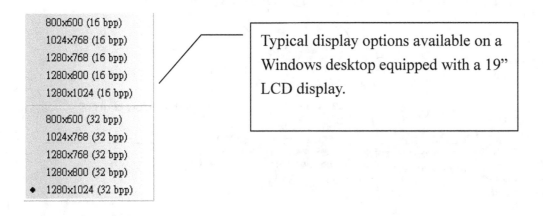

800x600 (16 bpp)
1024x768 (16 bpp)
1280x768 (16 bpp)
1280x800 (16 bpp)
1280x1024 (16 bpp)

800x600 (32 bpp)
1024x768 (32 bpp)
1280x768 (32 bpp)
1280x800 (32 bpp)
♦ 1280x1024 (32 bpp)

Typical display options available on a Windows desktop equipped with a 19" LCD display.

What is the optimal display resolution for the game to operate at runtime?

The higher the resolution the more workload your display card would have to handle. The good thing about a high resolution setting is that you can squeeze in more objects and let them interact with each others on the same screen. If your game involves movement of all these objects together, things will slow down significantly for sure. The game engine behind CONSTRUCT is NOT particularly fast in screen redraw!

If you prefer the game to run in windowed mode, through allowing the window to be stretched and have the window maximized at start the screen will be completely "filled up". There is no need to explicitly set any resolution mode. And there will be no change in the desktop resolution setting.

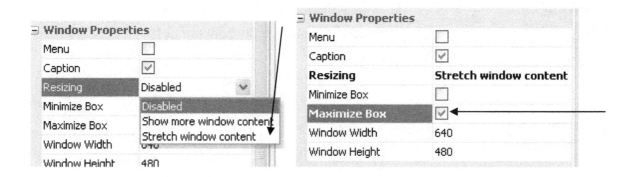

For the windowed mode to work you must disable the full screen option. If the full screen option is checked, all these window properties will become meaningless.

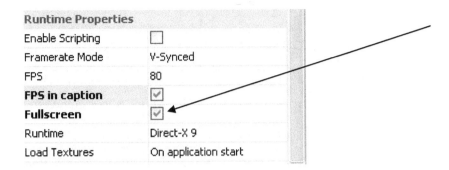

Performance-wise, full screen mode is usually the best. Therefore, if high frame rate is to be maintained, you should only use full screen mode.

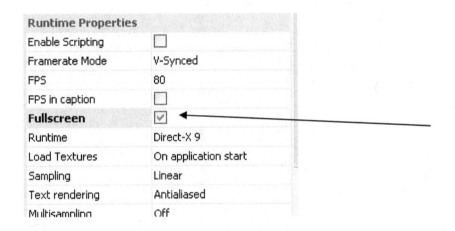

If you have a small window size and you choose to go full screen, the game engine will initiate a change in desktop resolution setting (a display mode change). This can produce problem on some desktop configurations (especially when the user presses ALT TAB to switch between the game and other running programs). For your interest, it is possible to set the display resolution and the display mode at runtime.

Construct : New action

Actions for 'System'

🔍

System ◁ ▷

Display

Scroll to X
Scroll to Y
Scroll to object
Set Motion Blur
Set display angle
Set display resolution ⟵
Set fullscreen
Set layout size
Set zoom

Construct : New action

Actions for 'System'

🔍

System ◁ ▷

Display

Scroll to X
Scroll to Y
Scroll to object
Set Motion Blur
Set display angle
Set display resolution
Set fullscreen ⟵
Set layout size
Set zoom

Construct : New action

Parameters for 'System - Set fullscreen'

🔍

Choose windowed or fullscreen mode.

Display mode

Windowed ▾ ⟵
Windowed
Fullscreen

C2 is a little bit different because the game built is in HTML5 and is supposed to run in a web browser window.

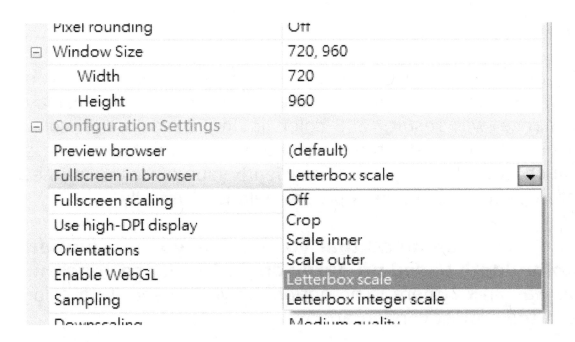

In fact, Window size which determines in pixels the size of the viewport is effective only if Fullscreen in browser is set to Off. You are recommended to try out different settings here.

What is the optimal color depth for the game to operate at runtime?

Talking about color-depth, the general theory is that when you have more color to display then slower overall display performance will result. 256-color is impractical (the color palette is way too restrictive). On the other hand, true-color is too much for the engine to efficiently sustain at runtime. Therefore, you must strike a proper balance carefully.

I would not recommend that you choose your resolution and color depth based primarily on performance concern. By the way, in C2 there is no option for you to specify a color mode in the project configuration:

⊟ Project settings	
First layout	(default)
Use loader layout	No
Pixel rounding	Off
⊞ Window Size	720, 960
⊟ Configuration Settings	
Preview browser	(default)
Fullscreen in browser	Letterbox scale
Fullscreen scaling	High quality
Use high-DPI display	Yes
Orientations	Any
Enable WebGL	On
Sampling	Linear
Downscaling	Medium quality
Physics engine	Box2D web
Loader style	Progress bar & logo
Pause on unfocus	No
Clear background	No

What is the role of DirectDraw? What frame rate setting

should I use?

CONSTRUCT performs 2D screen drawing operations primarily through the Microsoft DirectDraw API. This API is especially useful when you need your game to run in full screen mode. Runtime performance would largely depend on how DirectDraw performs under a particular resolution and color depth.

In theory, DirectDraw can use hardware acceleration if it is available on the hardware, even though the benefit is not dramatic. Some display card drivers are well written to take full advantage of DirectDraw, while some are not. In other words, performance can vary quite a bit across different computers.

You can pre-specify a target runtime frame rate. The higher the frame rate, the smoother the game goes. For 2D game, a framerate of 60 is generally sufficient.

Runtime Properties	
Enable Scripting	☐
Framerate Mode	V-Synced
FPS	80 ←
FPS in caption	☐

At runtime you can also specify a fixed frame rate. There is an action for this:

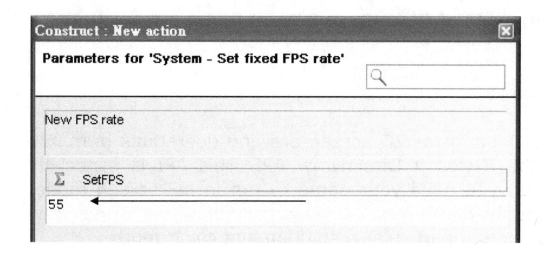

I prefer to leave the frame rate mode as-is. Although you can fix the frame rate, doing so can produce problem when the runtime computer is not capable of sustaining the target frame rate.

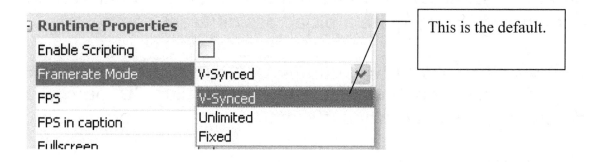

In C2, when you run a game in debug mode you can tell the frame rate per second:

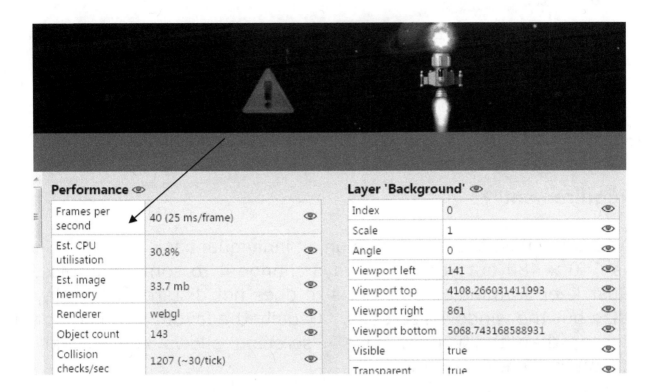

You can programmatically set the screen scaling via the Set fullscreen scaling action.

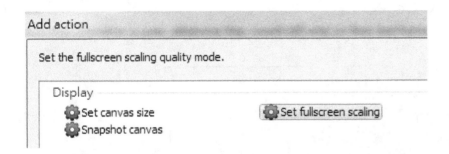

If you use high quality, of course the frame rate will be affected since the workload will be much heavier for the system.

Can I select different display modes for different game levels? How should I define the "minimum system requirement"?

You can adjust the layout size on an individual basis. The default is 640 x 480 but you can always change it to something else. Just keep in mind, the layout size does not dictate the display size but the window size does. Usually the layout size is much larger than the window size - scrolling allows you to walk through the entire layout.

Layout properties	
Name	Game
Event sheet	Game events
Active layer	FX
Unbounded scrolling	No
Layout Size	1024, 5120 ←
Width	1024
Height	5120
Margins	500, 500
Width	500
Height	500

Display mode should be configured at the application level. You should not try to use different display settings for different levels. A consistent display style is critical to the quality of your game.

If your target platform is Windows based PC, there isn't much to worry about in terms of "minimum requirement", since consumer desktop computers are so powerful and so cheap these days. Gamers don't live with slow machines. So don't let the minimum requirement concern restrict your creativity!

If you are using C2 to create games for platforms other than Windows PC, you must realize that the available horsepower is totally different.

BTW, layout scaling can be done programmatically:

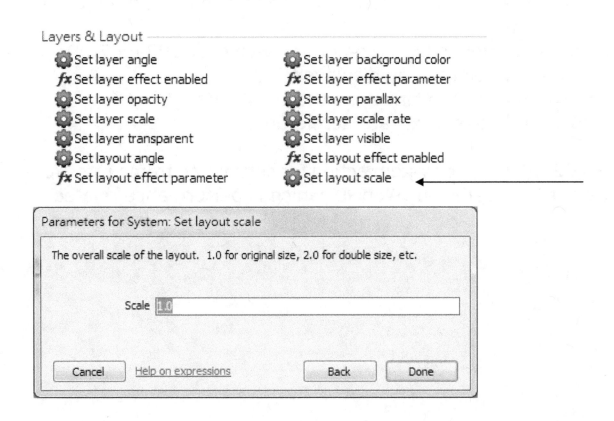

How to define and measure screen performance?

Frame rate is the key measure here. The more frames a game can sustain in any given time the smoother the screen display can go.

CONSTRUCT has a default frame rate configuration of 60. This is the frame rate you expect CONSTRUCT to deliver at runtime. You can adjust this value by hand at design time.

However, there are factors that work against this expectation:
- There are too many objects moving around on screen at the same time...
- The resolution is high (something well over 1024 x 768)
- Too many colors to be displayed
- Corrupted DirectX driver on the client side
- You don't have hardware acceleration

With C2, there is no system action for setting the frame rate. You do want to know about WebGL, which is performance related.

What is WebGL?

As a configuration setting, you may choose to enable WebGL.

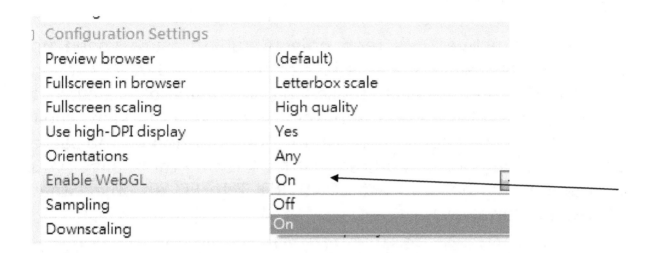

Simply put, it is a faster renderer.

HTML5 has a <canvas> tag which allows the game to run. There are two different ways to draw the game. The simple 2D context is slower but is less demanding in hardware.The WebGL context is based on OpenGL ES and is usually faster.

If you turn on WebGL and if it ends up fails to work, C2 will fall back to the simple mode automatically.

Can I improve screen performance by moving most active

objects off screen?

Having less active on-screen objects can for sure speed up screen redraw (since there is less to render). HOWEVER, even though off-screen objects (those waiting outside of the current window) are not rendered until they are actually in view, their existence can still cause performance degradation as the same amount of memory is required just for keeping them alive (you do have an option to direct CONSTRUCT to kill an object that moves too far away).

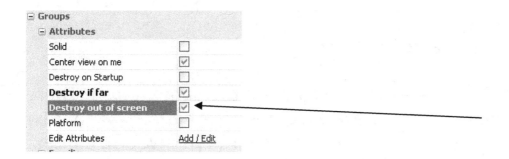

C2 has a behavior known as Destroy outside layout...

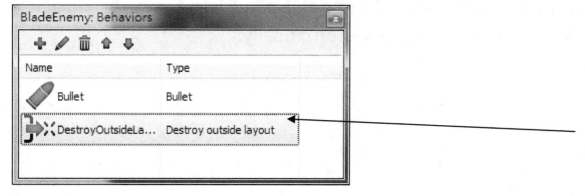

What are shaders and how do they work with the display

hardware in the context of CONSTRUCT?

Shaders are special programs capable of describing the traits of either a vertex or a pixel. A vertex shader deals with the position, texture coordinates, and colors of a vertex. A pixel shader, on the other hand, deals with the color, z depth and alpha value of a pixel. These programs can be used to modify graphical images at runtime such that special effects can be implemented.

Pixel shader is a very popular form of shader, which is often used for effects such as scene lighting, bump mapping and color toning.

On the Windows platform, shaders usually run with the help of Direct3D. Some shaders are programmed to work without strictly requiring hardware acceleration. However, how practical this can go without hardware help is quite questionable.

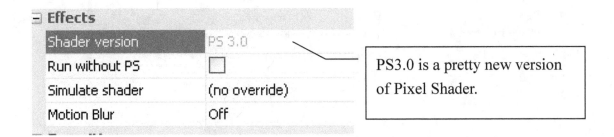

With PS2.0 or higher, special effect such as explosion can be blended nicely with the background using Screen blend. Without

PS, you will need to use Additive blend, which will not look as good.

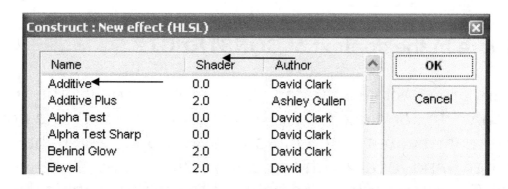

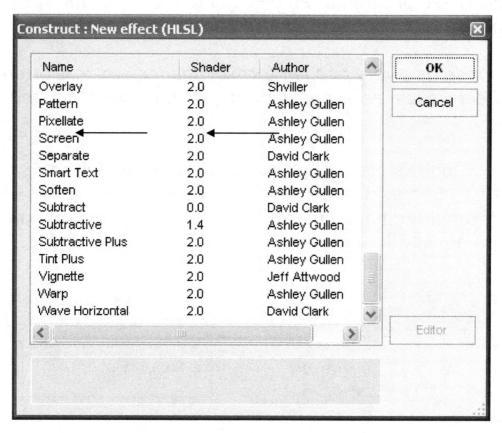

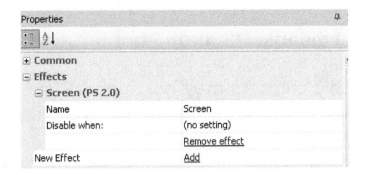

You can actually define an event condition to test for the available PS version at runtime:

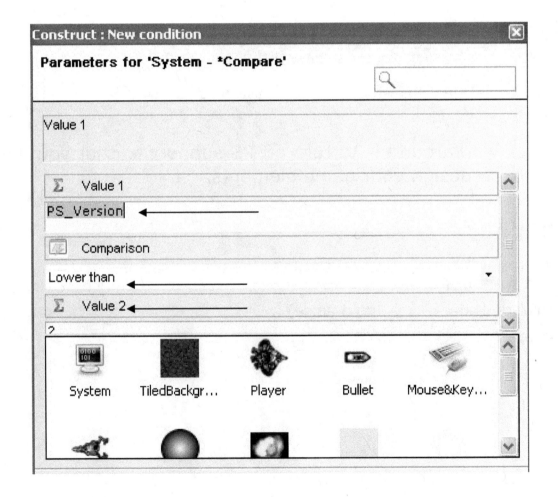

When should I disable PS altogether in CONSTRUCT?

All-in-one graphic chipsets may not support Pixel Shader. If PS support is turned on for your game, an error may occur:

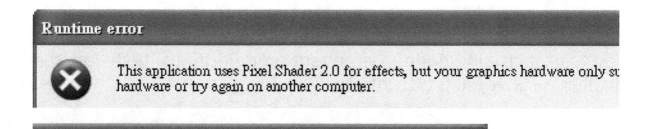

A quick workaround is to turn off PS support so that you don't have to re-design your game elements.

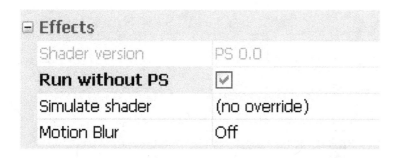

What is anti-aliasing all about?

Anti-aliasing refers to the technique of minimizing the distortion artifacts (the edgy look) when representing a high resolution image at a lower resolution or vice versa (which is quite common when an image is being resized). It works by blending the boundary pixels of the image in question. You can see a difference in display quality of textual data when this option is being manipulated (it does add workload to your display hardware).

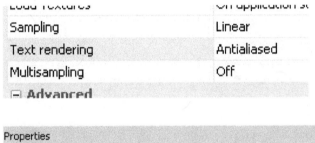

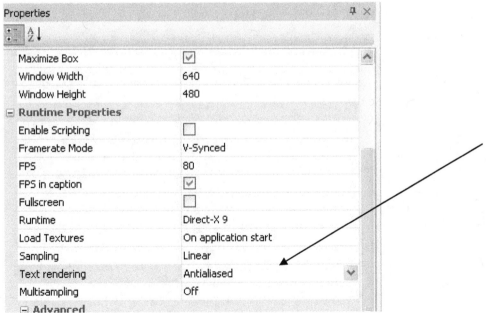

In C2, text object has a Blend Mode setting as well:

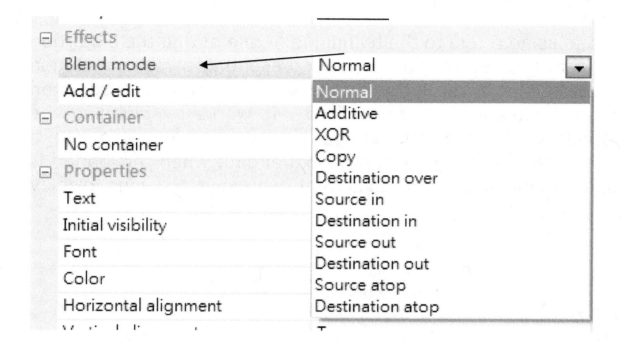

The setting is at the object level though.

What are the major runtime performance obstacles?

Assuming the computer and the OS are properly configured, major runtime performance obstacles of a CONSTRUCT game would include:

- stupidly complicated logics or endless loops, which keep the CPU busy doing computation all the time
- unrealistic screen details, which tax the display function heavily
- frequent disk write for saving game data, which involves disk access all the time

Most 2D action games shouldn't require intensive computation unless there is some serious flaw in the program logic. Unrealistic screen details and the extensive use of animation objects may slow things down and this is more or less a design issue. Disk write operations can be minimized by restricting the use of any "save game" mechanisms.

Game Design

Why would a single large object be counter-productive at

runtime?

In theory, a one-piece type large object is bad performance-wise. The primary problem is on screen redraw – a small tiny change somewhere on it would require that the whole object be redrawn. Redrawing a large object all the time is no fun at all.

Advances in computer hardware performance had made the rendering of very large objects a relatively less stressful process.

If you can break this single large object into multiple smaller objects, unnecessary screen redraw can be kept to an absolute minimum. *However, you need to define logics to link (or bind) these smaller objects together. The easiest thing to do is to define an event like this:*

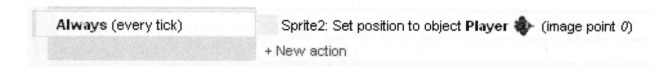

This event ties sprite2 to the position of image point 0 of the player sprite.

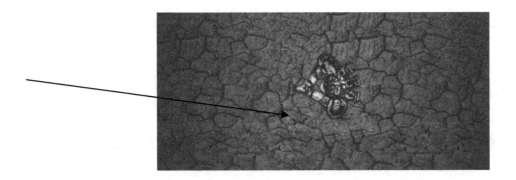

C2 has a feature known as Container, which allows you to use smaller objects to form a bigger object (they call it composite object).

Further information about this advanced feature can be found here:

https://www.scirra.com/manual/150/containers

What is the difference between a pivot point, an origin and

an image point? How to use them?

The pivot point of a sprite is by default the centre of the sprite object, which is also the axis for sprite rotation. This point is visible when you select a sprite in the layout editor:

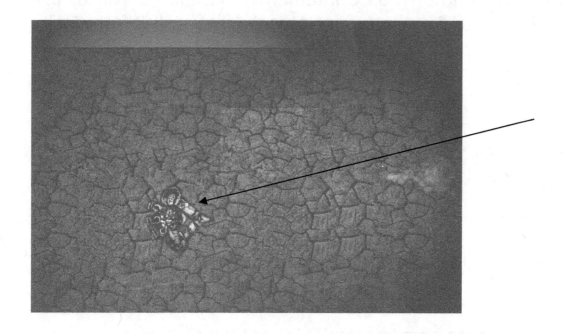

If there are spawn actions associated with the sprite (such as shooting bullet), newly spawned objects will be generated from the pivot point. Generally speaking you should not need to tamper with the pivot point setting.

An image point is visible in the picture editor. It is simply a point in the sprite image you can refer to. Instead of spawning bullets from the pivot point, you can specify that bullets be spawned from the image point. When editing an event you can also specify X Y location basing on the image point location.

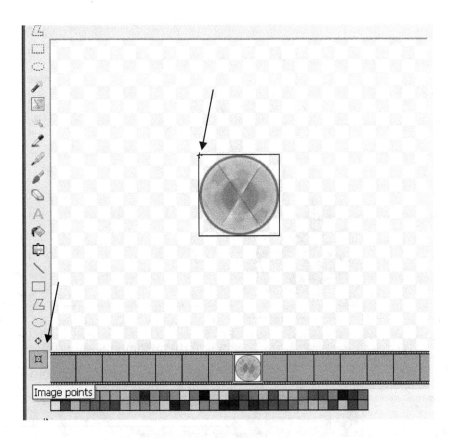

In the picture editor, you can specify multiple image points for a sprite, although they do not show up together at the same time.

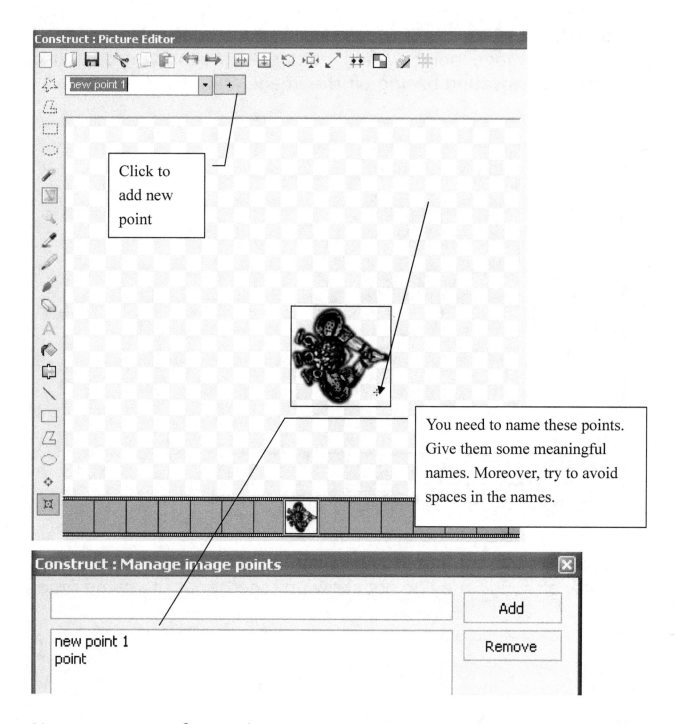

Construct : Picture Editor

new point 1

Click to
add new
point

You need to name these points.
Give them some meaningful
names. Moreover, try to avoid
spaces in the names.

Construct : Manage image points

Add

Remove

new point 1
point

Now you can refer to the image point when defining the event action.

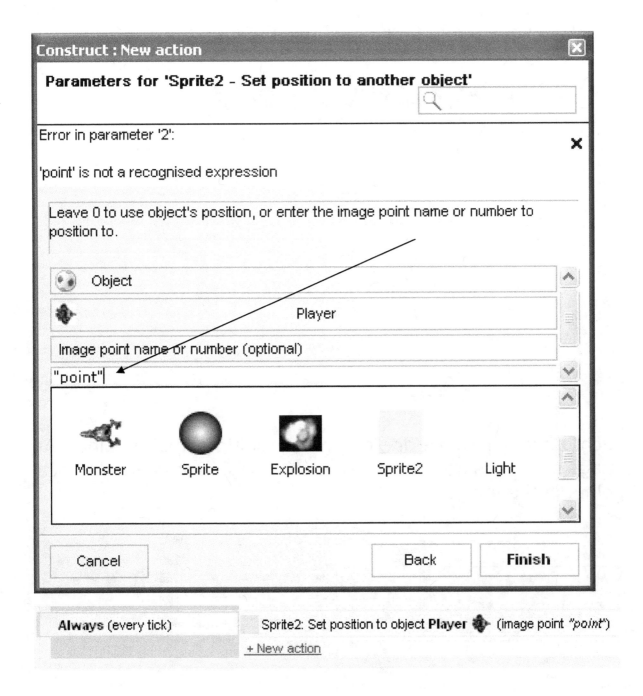

Construct : New action

Parameters for 'Sprite2 - Set position to another object'

Error in parameter '2':

'point' is not a recognised expression

Leave 0 to use object's position, or enter the image point name or number to position to.

Object

Player

Image point name or number (optional)

"point"

Monster   Sprite   Explosion   Sprite2   Light

Cancel   Back   **Finish**

Always (every tick)   Sprite2: Set position to object **Player** (image point *"point"*)

+ New action

In C2 we have origin and image points.

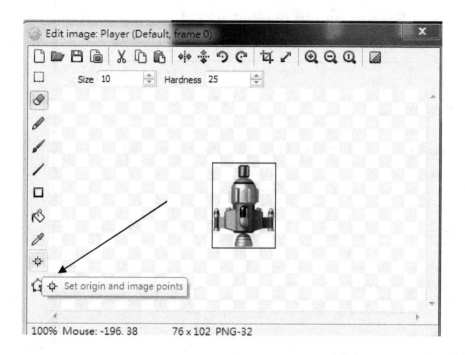

Each object can have one origin but multiple image points. An image's origin is its point of rotation. Image points are the focal points in the image.

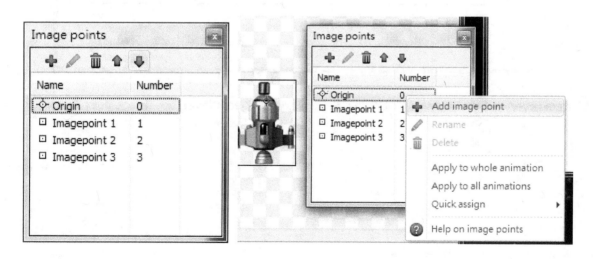

How to assign movement to a character sprite?

In CONSTRUCT, with a sprite selected you can add a behavior:

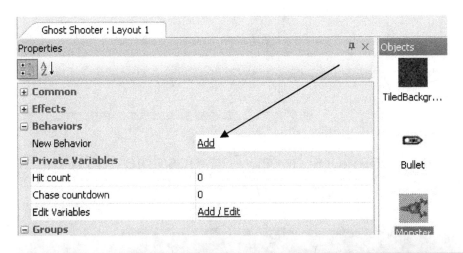

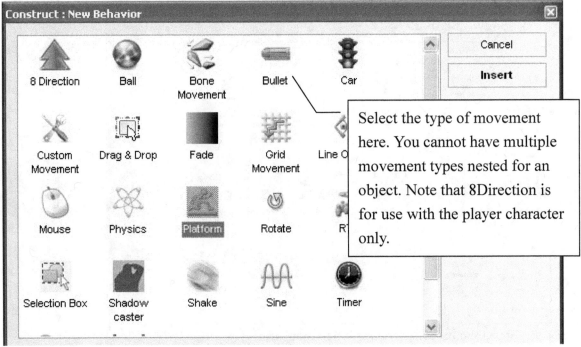

Select the type of movement here. You cannot have multiple movement types nested for an object. Note that 8Direction is for use with the player character only.

In C2, an object has a Behaviors section:

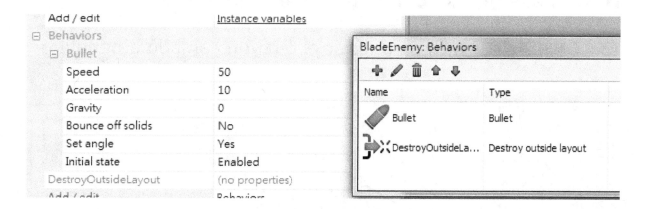

You can add or edit behaviors here. The possible movement types are shown below:

Can I have multiple 8Direction movements assigned to

different characters at the same time? Any alternative?

Yes you can. However, they will all respond to your movement commands together at the same time.

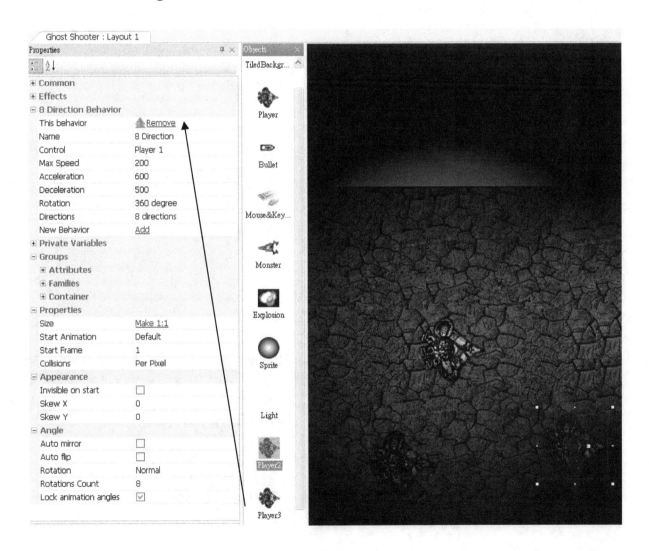

To allow a different character to act according to different inputs, you may need to use a keyboard related condition:

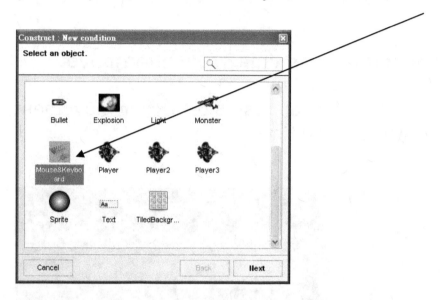

For example, when a key is pressed, the character sprite player 2 will move at a particular angle for a particular distance:

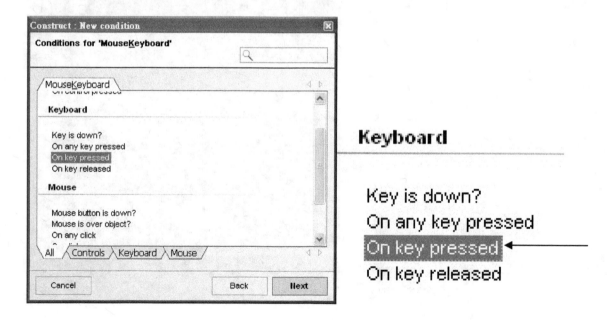

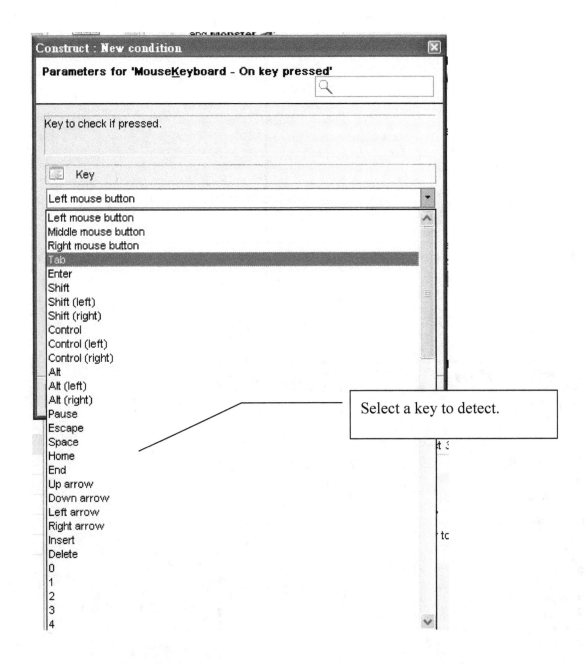

Select a key to detect.

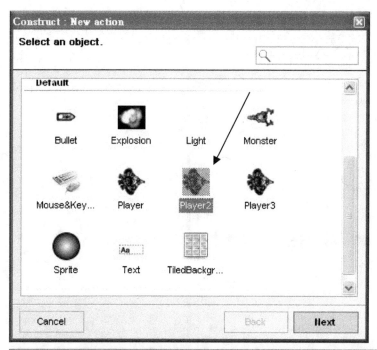

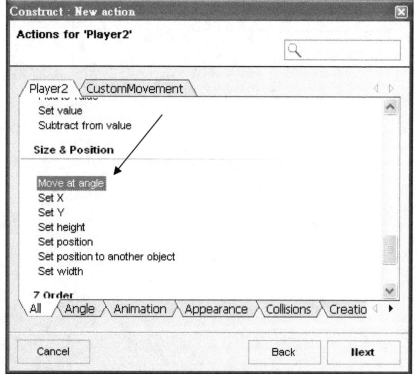

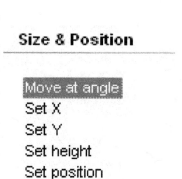

Size & Position

Move at angle
Set X
Set Y
Set height
Set position

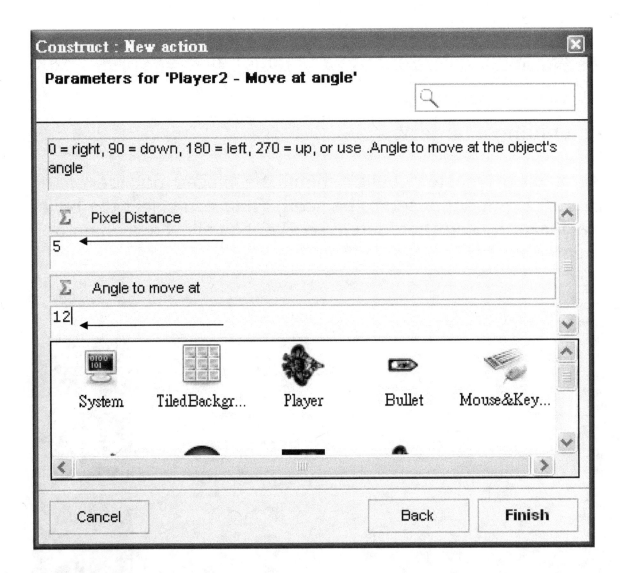

The same is true in C2. You can have multiple objects assigned with 8direction, just that it would not make sense at all to do so.

How to assign movement to a bullet character sprite? How about hitting a target?

First of all a "master" bullet should be placed outside of the layout. It is not supposed to be seen. Then you select the bullet behavior for it, and then define an event to allow spawning of it from another sprite (such as from the player character or from a gun).

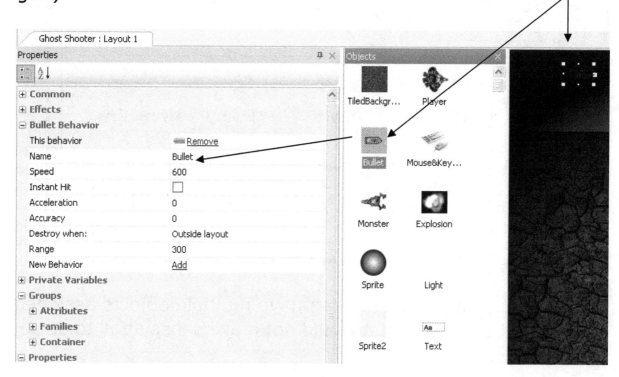

When the left mouse is clicked, the bullet is spawn from the player character:

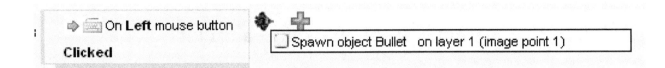

When the bullet hits the target, the target's health count is decremented.

When the bullet collides with the monster, add to its hit count, and create an explosion and light.

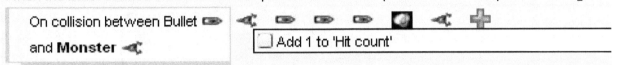

An explosion object is spawned from the bullet.

When the bullet collides with the monster, add to its hit count, and create an explosion and light.

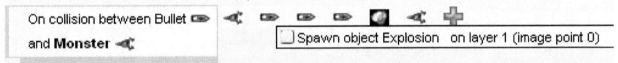

After that, the bullet (only this particular bullet, NOT the master bullet) is destroyed.

When the bullet collides with the monster, add to its hit count, and create an explosion and light.

C2 has bullet shooting implemented similarly.

What is the correct way of spawning a bullet?

Say you want the player object to shoot the bullet. Assuming the player sprite has the proper image point defined, from the event work sheet you do the following:

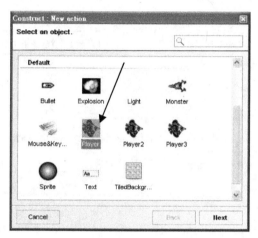

Select the player sprite.

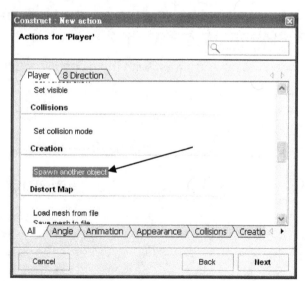

Select "spawn another object".

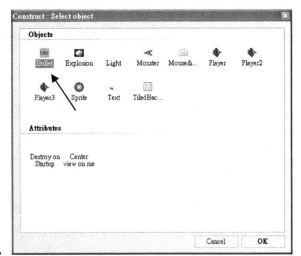

Select the desired bullet object.

Spawning means creating a new object out of it. If you are using C2, you define the object involved, the layer it resides on, and the relevant image point to use.

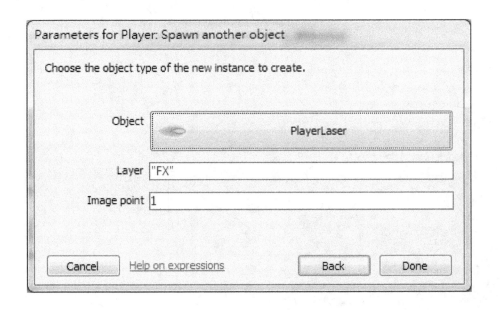

How to ensure that the "master" bullet and other "master" objects" that were placed outside will not be visible?

The best way is to ensure your player will not be able to walk outside of the layout. This has to do with restriction on screen scrolling. When the unbounded scrolling option is enabled, the player will be able to scroll to the edges, making things outside of the layout visible.

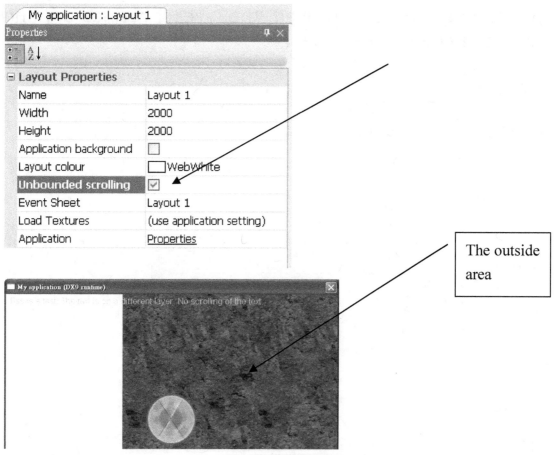

The outside area

My recommendation is that you should always leave the unbounded scrolling option unchecked.

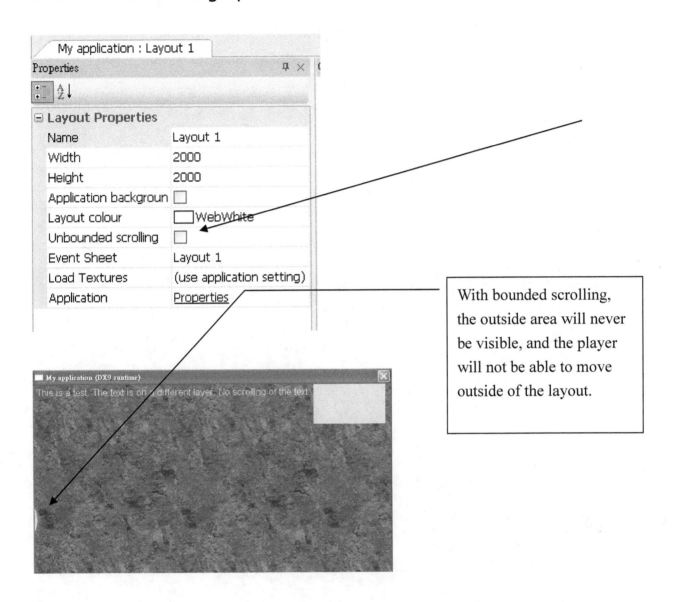

With bounded scrolling, the outside area will never be visible, and the player will not be able to move outside of the layout.

In C2, unbounded scrolling is a layout properties option.

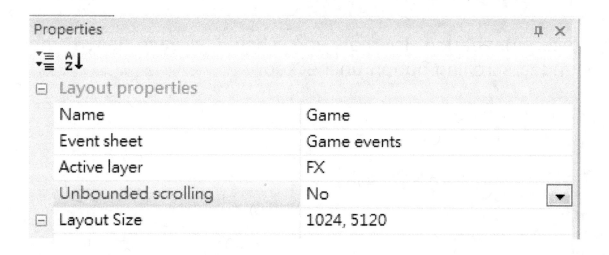

How do I allow for multiple bullets to be propelled towards different directions at the same time?

You can spawn bullets from different image points (if you have defined multiple image points for the player).

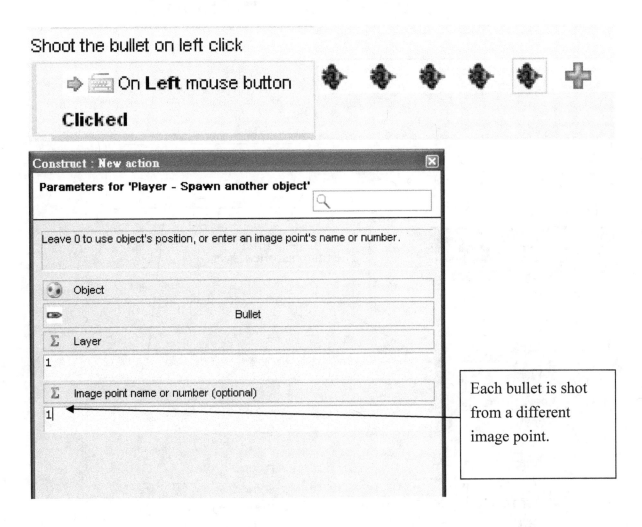

Each bullet is shot from a different image point.

Why should I implement multiple layers?

Say your game allows scrolling, and you want some dashboard items (score, health ...etc) to be presented on the screen. You can implement scrolling on one layer, and then present the dashboard stuff on another layer that has no scrolling allowed.

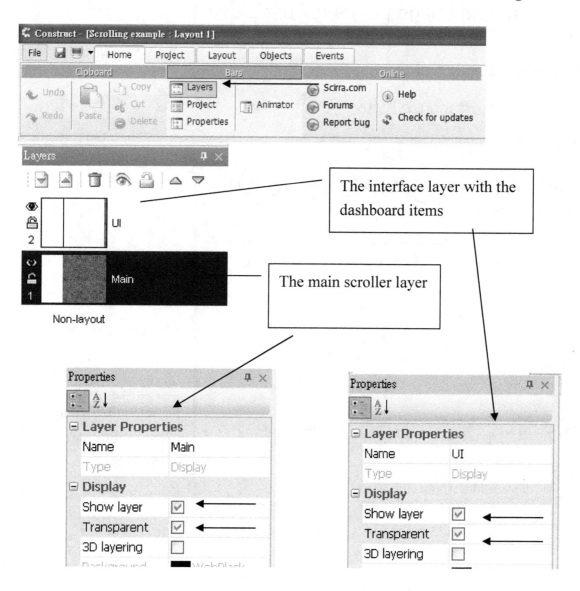

"No scrolling" can be accomplished easily by setting the scroll X rate and the scroll Y rate of a layer to 0.

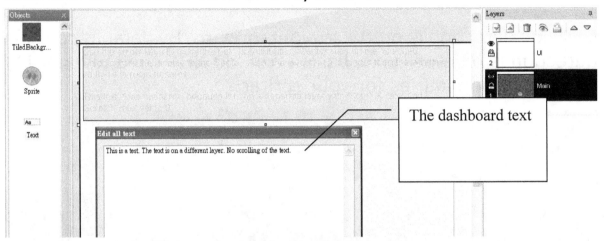

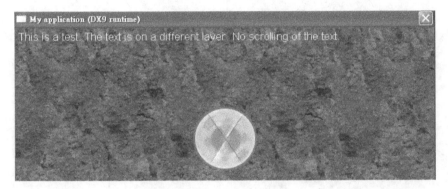

Sometimes you may need to arrange the display order of layers in order for certain items to be displayed. The up and down arrows on the right can be used for this purpose.

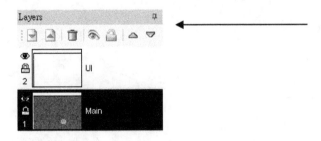

Collision detection on the same layer...

Collision detection is pretty straight forward. By default, collision detection is on a per pixel basis – you do NOT need to explicitly define any boundaries for your sprites.

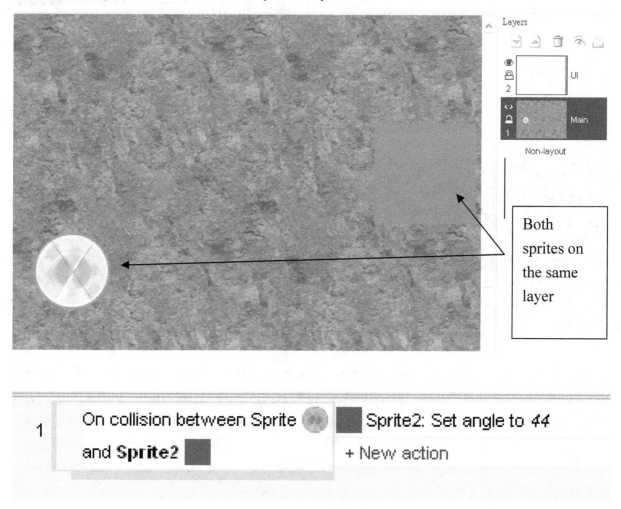

Copyright 2015. **The HobbyPRESS (Hong Kong)**. All rights reserved.

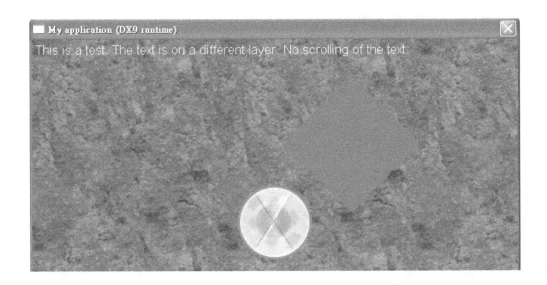

This is a test. The text is on a different layer. No scrolling of the text.

In fact it is always recommended that you use the default. Say the player is round shaped. If you use any rectangular boundary for collision detection, the outcome will become inaccurate.

The picture editor allows you to define special collision mask for a sprite. Generally speaking you should not need to use this feature.

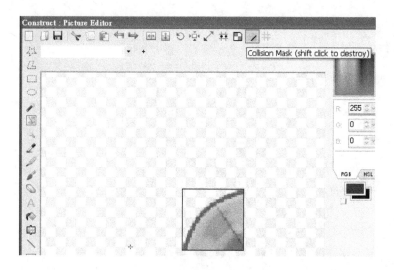

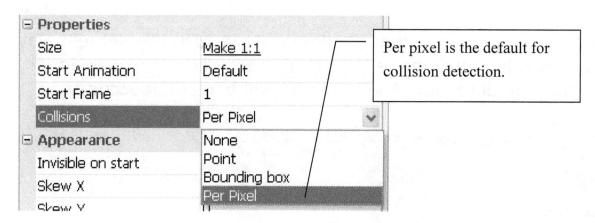

Per pixel is the default for collision detection.

C2, on the other hand, allows the fine tuning of collision polygon. Also, collision is enabled or disabled on a per object basis.

Collision detection across different layers...

Collision detection across layer is automatic, nothing special needs to be done to enable it.

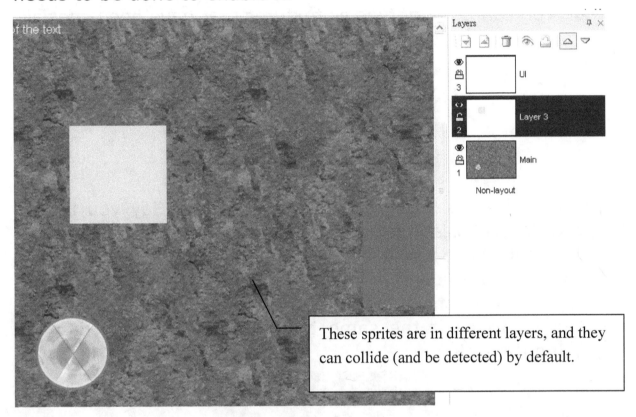

These sprites are in different layers, and they can collide (and be detected) by default.

What is special about background tiling?

If you are doing backgrounds, the traditional technique is to use tiles. Properly designed tiles have patterns that look extremely well. *You can think of tiles as textures that have been specially formatted to blend together really well.*

The logic behind background tiling is simple. Say you have a background consisting of one huge brick wall. Using one single big bitmap for it would be a waste of memory UNLESS each single brick of the wall is unique. If the bricks are more or less the same, a memory-saving method of building up such wall would be to paint the same brick repetitively on screen for forming the wall.

These walls can be "built" pretty easily by the repetitive use of the same brick piece.

The general advice out there for background tiles is to make tile units in pixel squares of no larger than 256x256 for efficient processing to take place on the computer without sacrificing visual quality (power-of-2 texture sizes such as 2, 4, 16, 128 …etc are usually the best).

In CONSTRUCT, configuring tiled background is easy. Just get the tile bitmap ready, then specify the area size. Tiling will then be completed automatically.

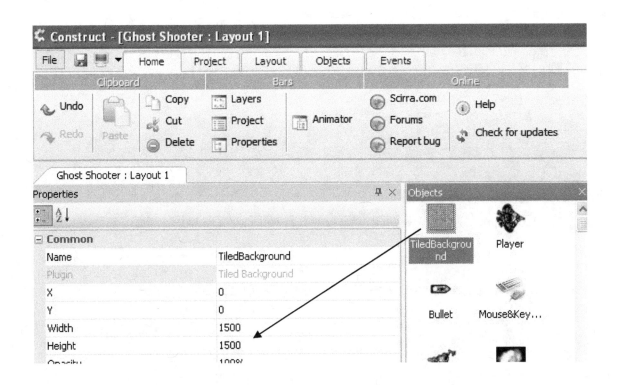

In C2, tiled background is an object you can place onto a layer:

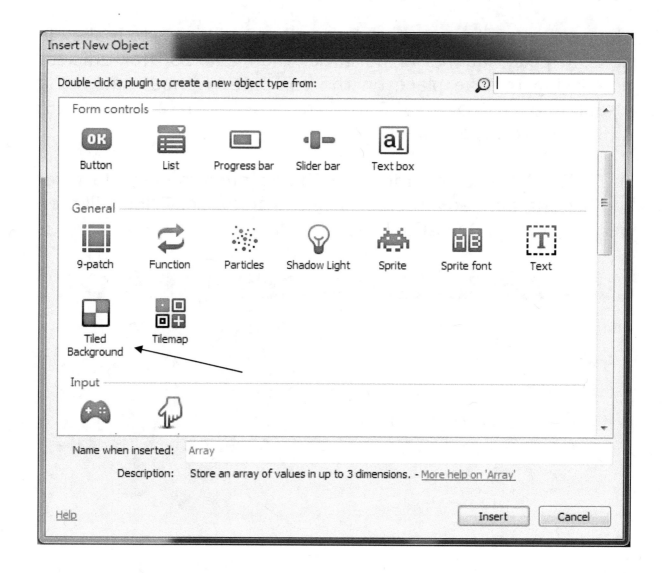

A single large object VS a group of smaller objects linked

together: a design time decision?

Say you need to create a big boss, which is a large tank like spaceship with 3 tank turrets capable of shooting in different directions. If you create this big boss as a single active object, all graphics and animations must be created as a whole, and the actions of the 3 turrets must be pre-planned. If the boss is to react to your attack, the 3 turrets will have to react together in a pre-defined manner since they all belong to the same object. Such design is simple and straight forward, and you will unlikely run into bugs. Flexibility and controllability are lacking though.

If instead of making it as a single object you come up with a 4-piece design consisting of the spaceship object, the turretA object, the turretB object and the turretC object. Now you can have individual control over each essential part of the big boss, since each object can have different actions for reacting to different event conditions. Visually, you can "link" them together simply by manipulating their positions and their animation sequences through the event work sheet (say, turretA must always be in a position which is X,Y to the spaceship object).

See this massive scale spaceship with lots of individual turrets on it? Each of these turrets can shoot and be hit on an individual basis. Therefore they should be implemented as individual active objects "bound" to the main spaceship body.

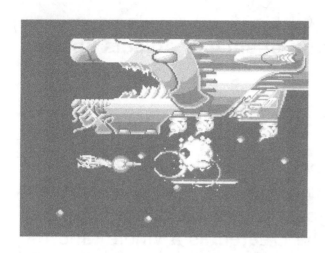

This approach gives flexibility and controllability. HOWEVER, it may just be outright improper for certain types of enemy character. Say if the big boss is a Godzilla, how would you link the head, body, tail, and craws together satisfactorily?

Remember the big boss in R-Type? With a boss of this size and complexity I would definitely implement it with at least three different objects – the head, the body and the tail. In fact, given the complexity and nature of the tail I may even consider to "assemble" the tail from multiple smaller objects!

More on "binding" objects together...

Mario needs to ride on the dinosaur. That means the two objects must first collide and overlap with each other. The event will need to cover this condition, plus any other special condition (such as pressing a particular key).

Once the intention to ride is confirmed through meeting these conditions, the two objects can play their corresponding special animation sequences (to make it look like Mario is actually riding on the dinosaur). The dinosaur can also be bound to Mario (through relative positioning) so that Mario is in control of all the movement. What that means is that Mario is still doing all the actual running and jumping (probably with increased speed and strength), but just that it looks like it is the dinosaur that handles all the tough works.

An event may be put in place such that when the couple receives a hit, Mario will get knocked off and the binding broken. *In any case the two would remain as separate objects at all time.*

Configuring big bosses for your levels

As previously said, some big bosses are better to be created and animated in a one-piece form. Say you have a Godzilla monster. You want to configure it in such a way that its head is weaker than its belly. In other words, a hit on the head is going to hurt more and let it scream differently.

An easy way to do this is to make use of several transparent dummy objects. Have these objects bound to the corresponding body parts of the Godzilla. They take the hits and react on behalf of the true Godzilla body. Because they are separate objects, you can configure each of them differently and uniquely. Once the predefined total hit threshold is reached, an event can trigger an action to terminate the Godzilla.

The effective use of transparent dummy objects can make game creation easier and more manageable!

C2 provides a useful feature known as container. It is an advanced feature and the relevant official documentation can be found here:

https://www.scirra.com/manual/150/containers

How to use private variable in CONSTRUCT?

An object can have its own private variables. You use private variables to keep track of things, such as life, health, score ...etc.

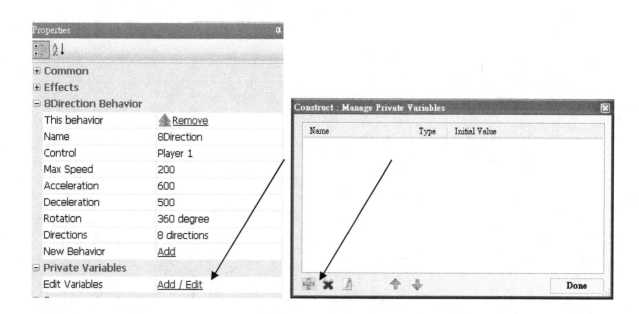

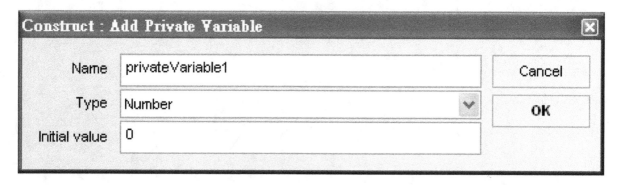

The variables defined can be used in event conditions / actions accordingly. They are most useful as numbers, for counting/discounting values.

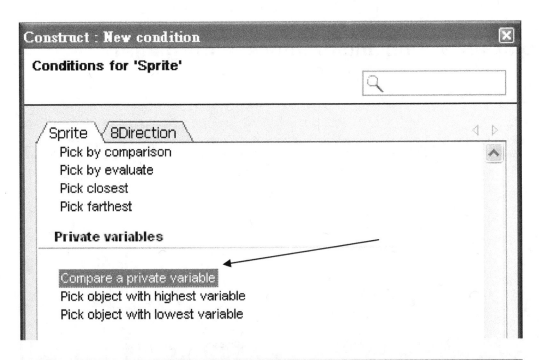

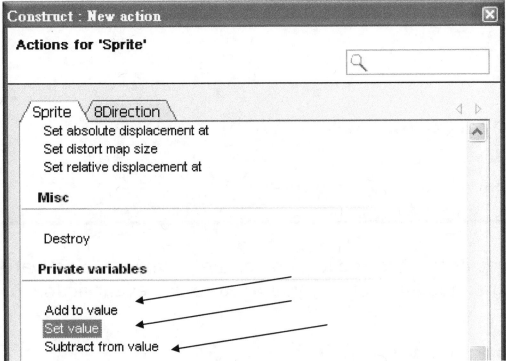

* In C2, private variables are instance variables.

How to play animation and/or movie in the game?

You can use the AVI object.

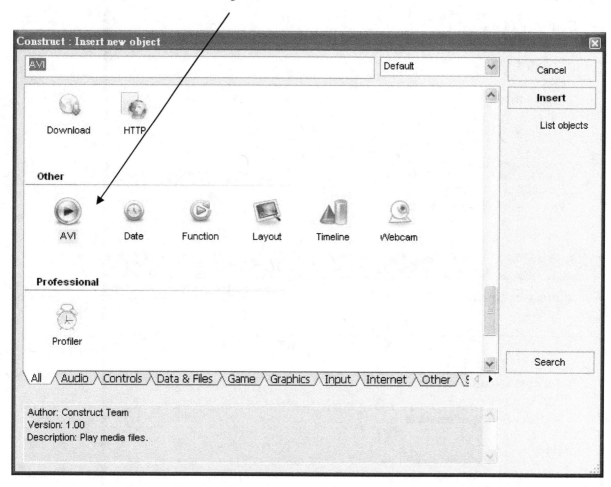

You can specify the size and location of the playback. To activate the playing and loading of file, you need to use event action.

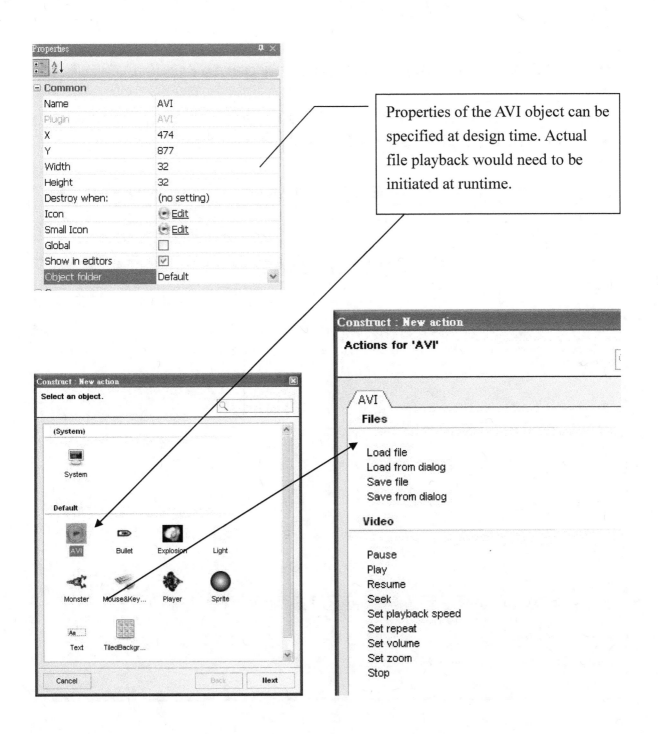

Properties of the AVI object can be specified at design time. Actual file playback would need to be initiated at runtime.

How to play sound and music in the game?

In CONSTRUCT you should use the XAudio2 object. Do NOT use the Directsound object since it is rather outdated.

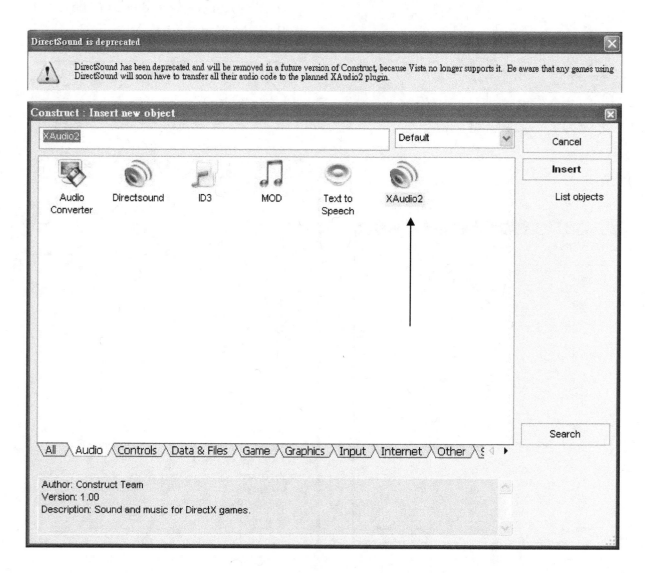

Copyright 2015. **The HobbyPRESS (Hong Kong)**. All rights reserved.

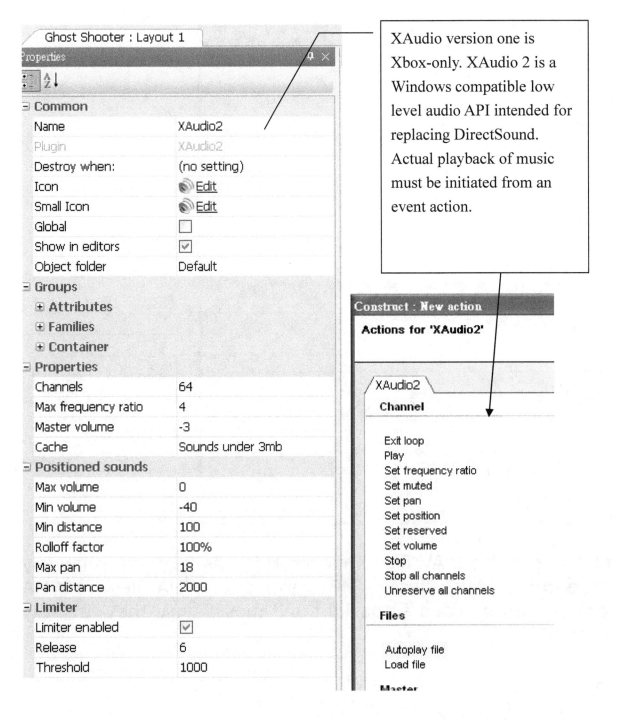

XAudio version one is Xbox-only. XAudio 2 is a Windows compatible low level audio API intended for replacing DirectSound. Actual playback of music must be initiated from an event action.

The most popular sound format to use with XAudio2 is WAV.

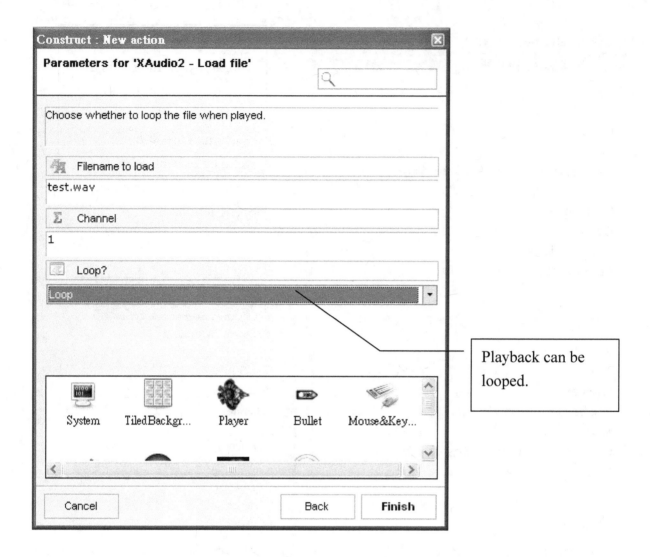

Playback can be looped.

You do not use WAV files for everything as they are relatively large in size. MP3 files (in MP3 format) or WMA files (in WMA format) can be used as background music since they are way smaller.

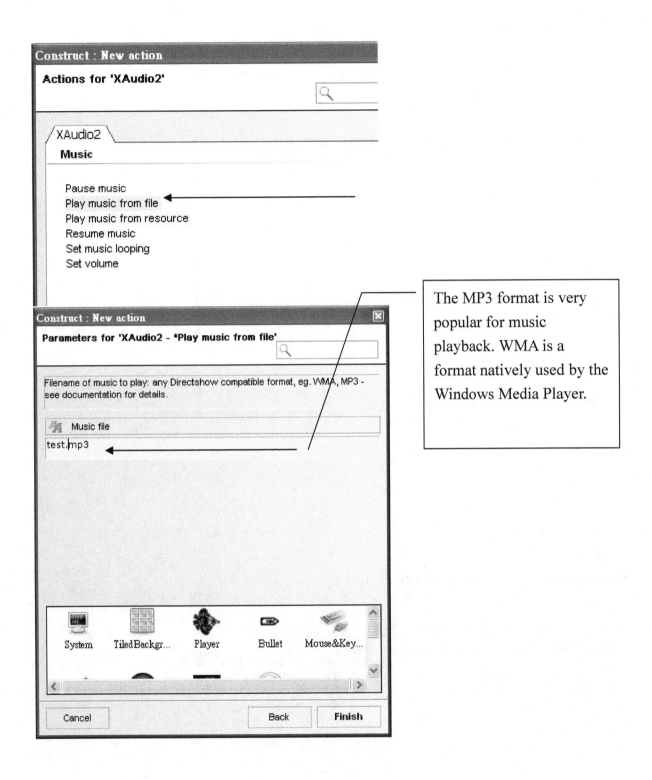

The MP3 format is very popular for music playback. WMA is a format natively used by the Windows Media Player.

With C2 you use the Audio object. You insert this object into the project, then import sound files by right clicking the Sounds folder accordingly.

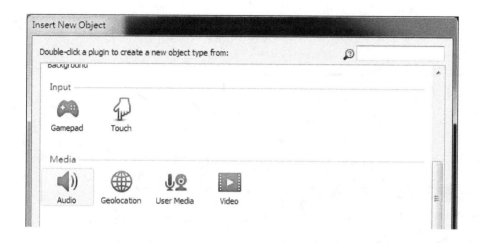

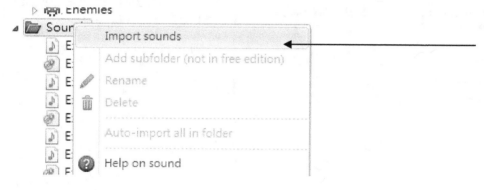

Many file formats are supported:

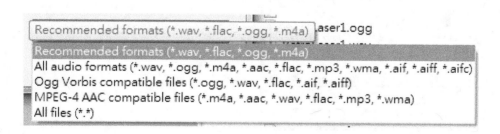

The fancy way of carrying a weapon

When your character is small, the action of holding and shooting a gun by the player object is usually done in one-piece with different animation sequences.

When the character is big (and when you want to allow for fancy operations such as exchanging/swapping weapons with other objects, weapon damage when getting hits ...etc), it may be a good idea for the weapon to be implemented as a separate object.

The weapon can be bound to the player's location or image point, and actual shooting can be done by the weapon itself (it takes player command directly by "listening" to keyboard events).

Screen scrolling effect creation

When you create a layout, you need to define the width and the height. If, say, this is a platform game with scrolling solely taking place horizontally, you can either scroll the layout or keep the layout static but scroll the background objects.

Special effects can be created by having different groups of background objects (such as clouds) moving at different speed, producing the effect of parallaxing - that is, when parts of the screen scroll faster than the rest.

For example, by adding a bullet behavior to the cloud sprite and set the bullet speed to something slower than the default, you can create a realistic sky scrolling effect. You can place different cloud sprites on different layers, then adjust the opacity and the bullet speed as needed.

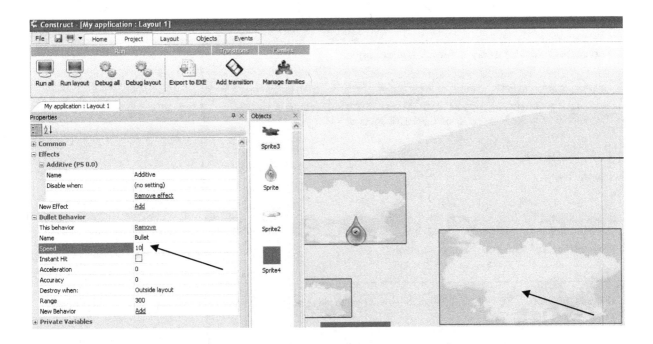

An alternative method is to set the cloud sprite to move towards an angle for a distance every *n* milliseconds.

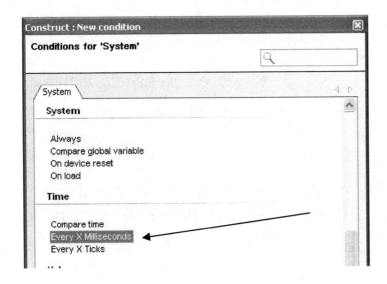

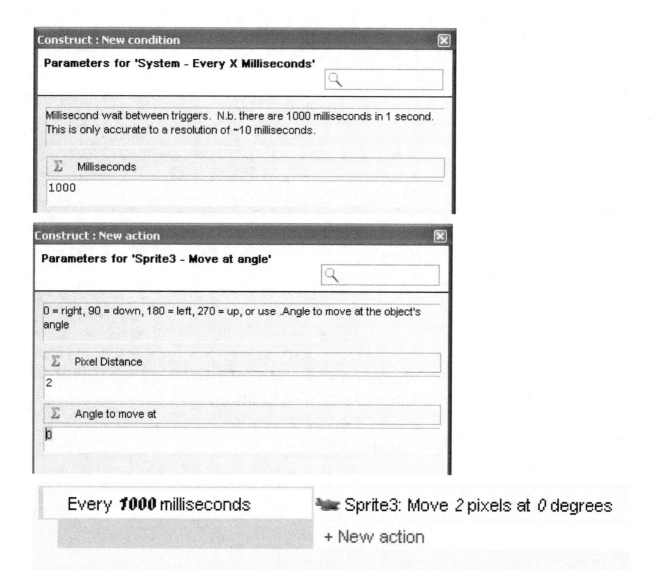

You do need to keep in mind, moving a large number of background objects across the screen simultaneously can be inefficient. Therefore, use this method only after careful assessment.

With Construct, screen scrolling can be implemented easily by the simple "center view on me" method. As long as you have a large layout (one larger than the window) and "center view on me" enabled on one character, the view will follow this character automatically.

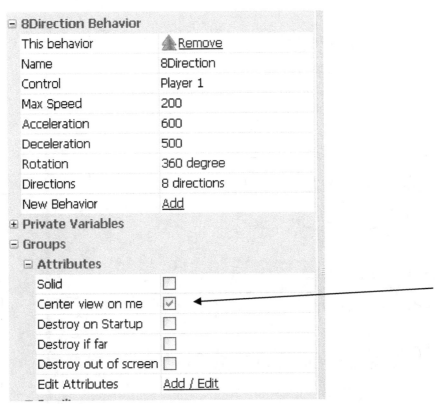

The straightforward way is to have the view chasing the player. If the game is a scroller, you may define a special dummy character (an invisible one) for the view to chase.

You can apply "center view on me" on different objects. HOWEVER, only one will be effective at runtime. It does not matter where these objects reside – even if they are in different layers, only one will be effective for "leading" the view. In fact, you can define the object to scroll to at runtime as well:

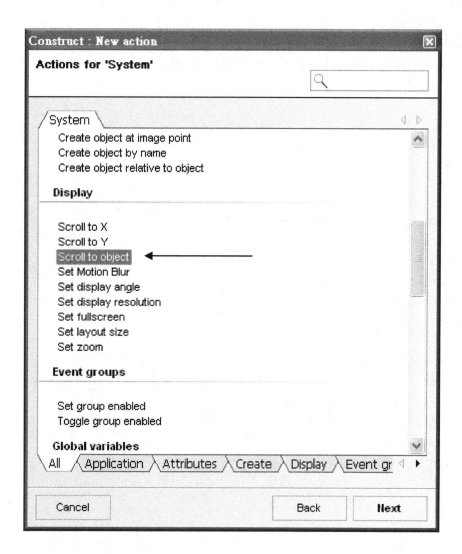

Scrolling speed is a per layer setting. You can pre-adjust the scroll X rate and the scroll Y rate of a layer at design time. If both are set to 0, no scrolling for that particular layer will take place. The X Y rates do not have to be the same. You can also manipulate them at runtime.

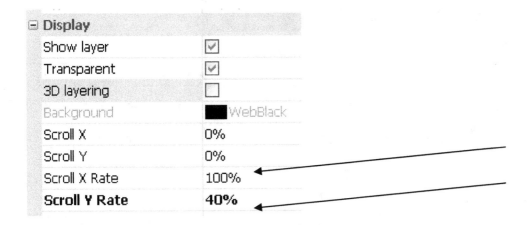

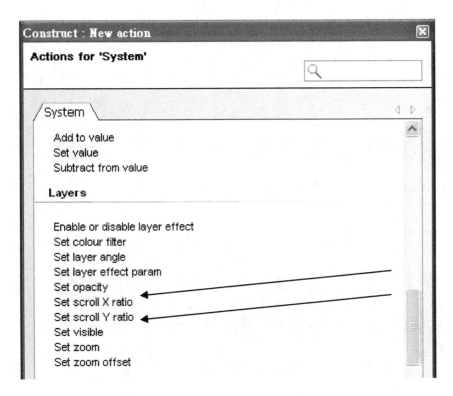

Copyright 2015. **The HobbyPRESS (Hong Kong)**. All rights reserved.

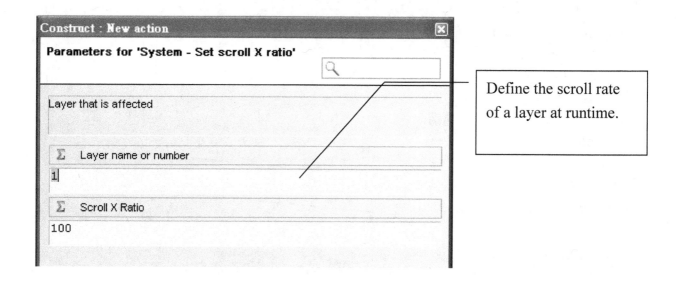

Define the scroll rate of a layer at runtime.

C2 has a template autorunner project you can study to learn how proper scrolling works in C2:

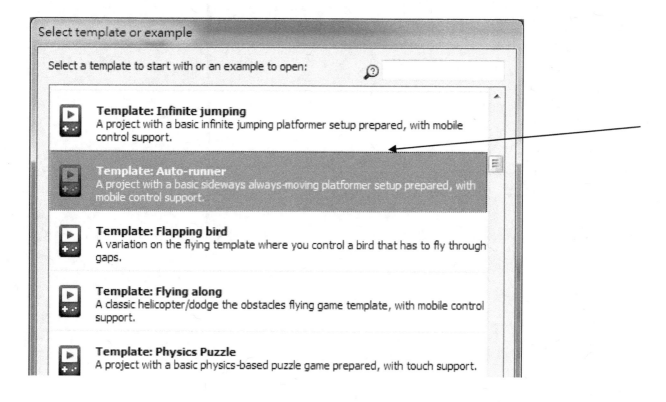

Copyright 2015. **The HobbyPRESS (Hong Kong)**. All rights reserved.

FYI, in C2 there is a system action called Set layer paralax:

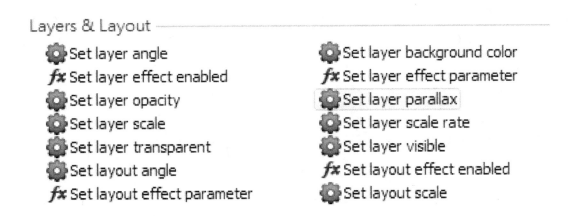

You can adjust the X and Y scrolling of a particular layer independently.

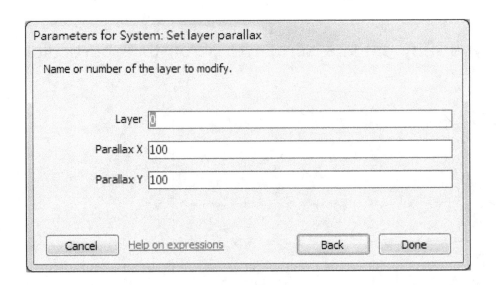

There are also system actions on scrolling:

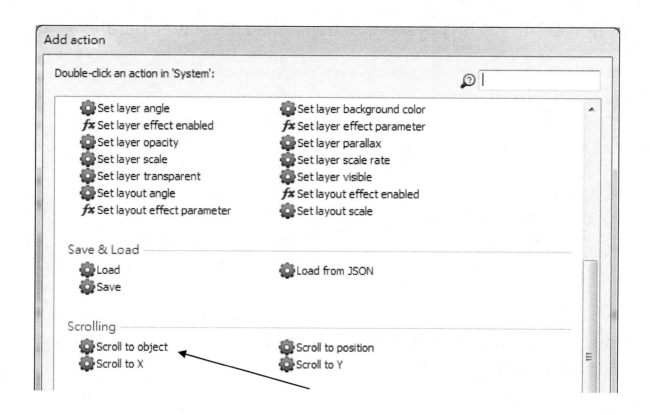

For example, you may set the screen to scroll to a particular object:

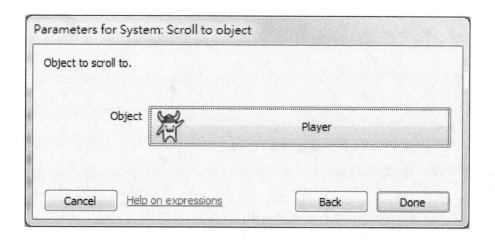

Platformer creation

Creating Mario brothers kind of platformer is fairly easy. For the platform bricks, all you need are sprites with the solid attribute turned on.

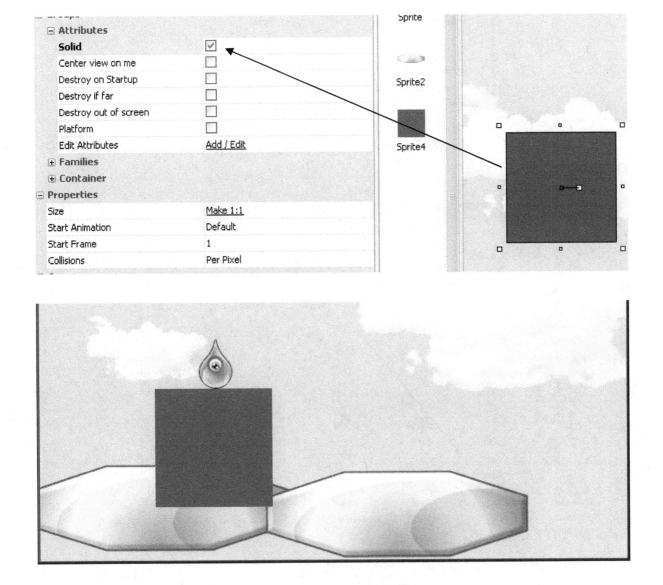

For the player, instead of 8direction you need to use the platform behavior.

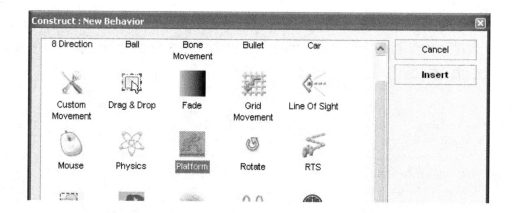

This behavior adds gravity to the player character. C2 platform behavior is similar:

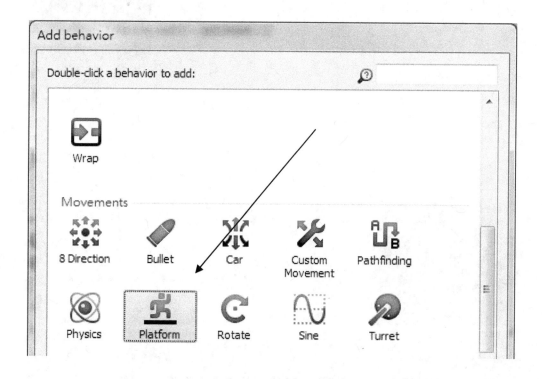

Is it a bad idea to construct a very large level in the game?

Talking about the size of a level, you want to know the difference between storage size and memory consumption. A very sophisticated game with many large levels and fancy objects will have a very large physical size. That means it can easily occupy a CD or even a DVD. But who cares? A DVD is so cheap to produce, that size in this regard just doesn't produce any problem.

The CONSTRUCT engine will NOT load the entire game into memory for execution. It will load only the current active level into memory. Therefore, a large total physical size of the entire game on disk does not really matter (if your worry is on memory consumption).

Depending on how you build your level (the number and size of objects, the amount and complexity of logics ...etc), memory consumption can be fine tuned as needed. If you want to build a large fancy world in your game, a smart thing to do would be to break it down into multiple smaller worlds. It is all about modular design – smaller worlds are always easier to manage and maintain ☺. You can "link" multiple smaller layouts together via an event action, which allows you to jump back and forth between game levels.

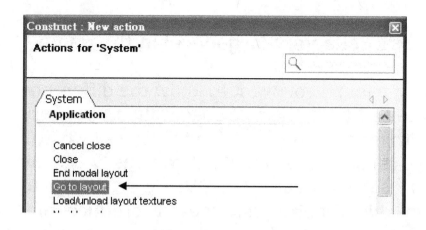

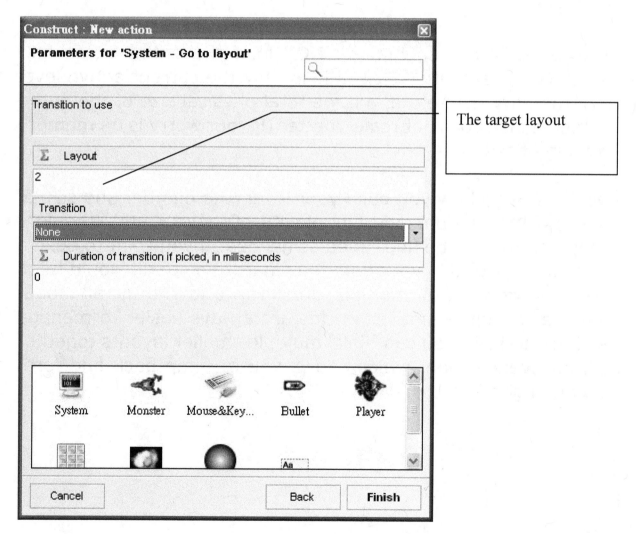

The target layout

Copyright 2015. **The HobbyPRESS (Hong Kong)**. All rights reserved.

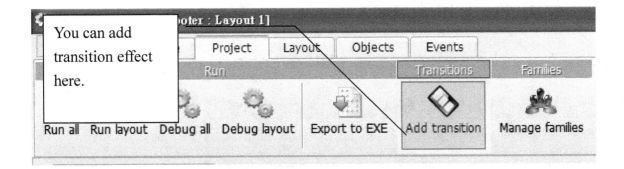

You can add transition effect here.

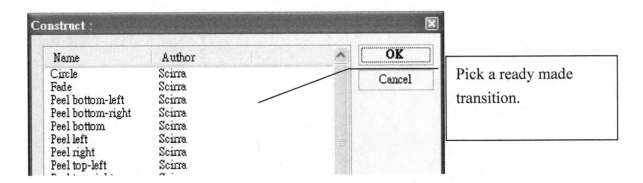

Pick a ready made transition.

C2 also has a system action known as Go to layout:

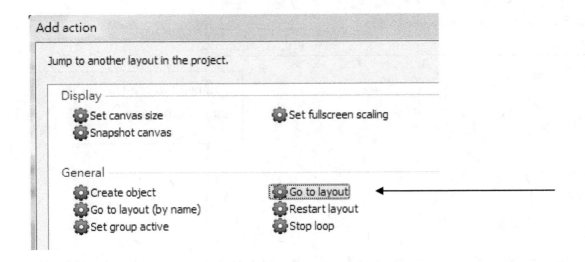

What action can be used to save and load game data?

You can use the save/load to disk event action:

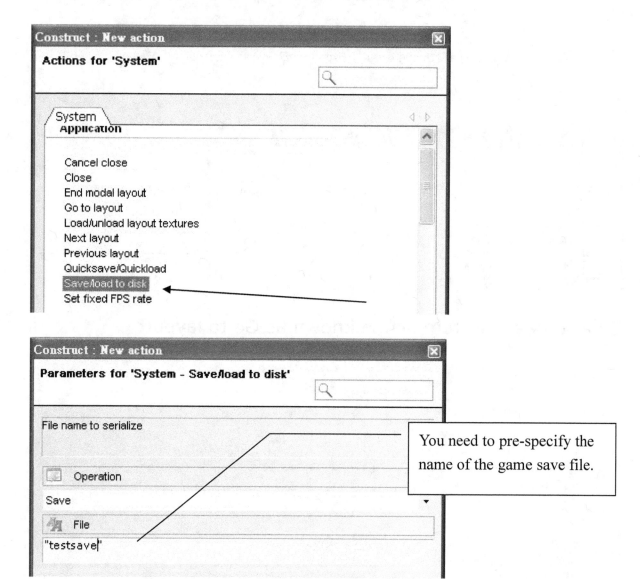

This file is binary, and is readable only through the load action.

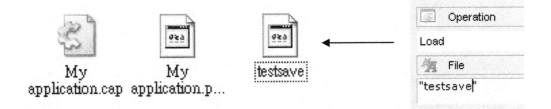

C2 also allows the saving of game data via System action:

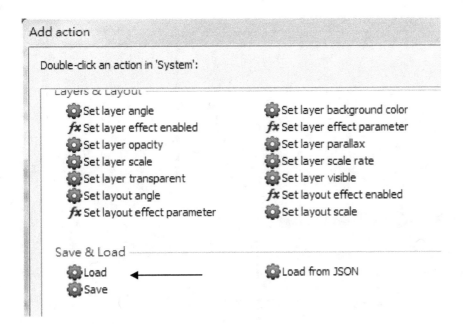

You do need to specify a string to identify the game state:

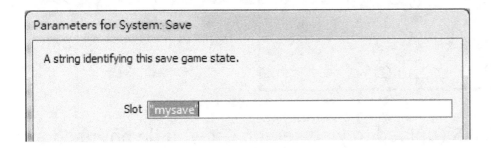

How can I make installation of my standalone game easier?

CONSTRUCT provides basic installer functionality at the time you export your project to an EXE file.

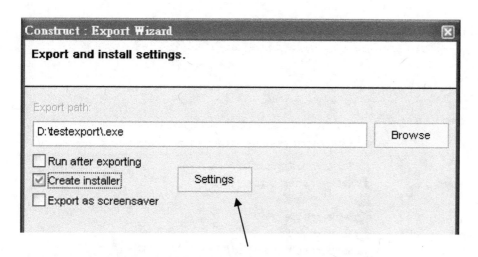

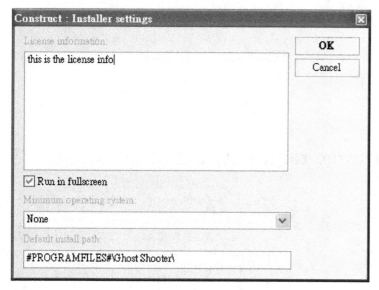

C2 targets HTML5 (upload to web server) so you do not need an installer.

Everything C2 is HTML5. The problem with this is that it is not in a form of downloadable executable, therefore charging $ for download becomes uneasy.

Fortunately, there is one thing called NWJS, which is sort of like a freely redistributable Chromium browser that can be used to hold and run your HTML5 game. Technically speaking, it is a framework for building desktop applications with HTML, CSS, and JavaScript. It allows a HTML5 based application to load a local web site within an application window while interacting with the Operating System via a JavaScript API.

C2 has an option for exporting a project to Desktop – NW.js:

However, you need to separately download the NW.js component from Scirra and have it installed on your computer. Our test setup involves this file:

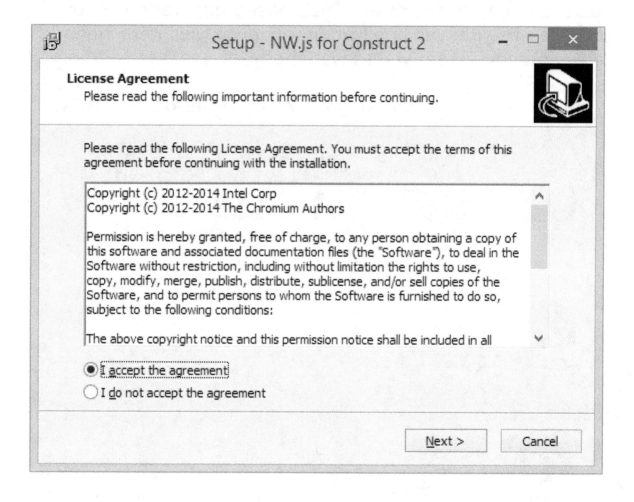 nwjs-for-c2-v0-17-0

NW.js is a product made available through Intel, and you need to agree to their terms in order to proceed:

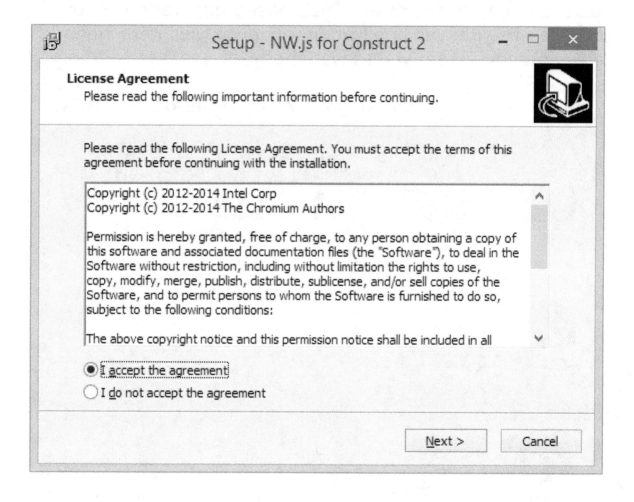

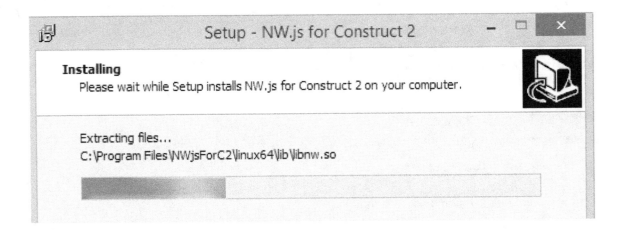

Certain DirectX components are required, so if you don't have them you can ask the installer to do it for you:

When you go ahead and export, the ability to compress and minimize scripts are optional even though recommended.

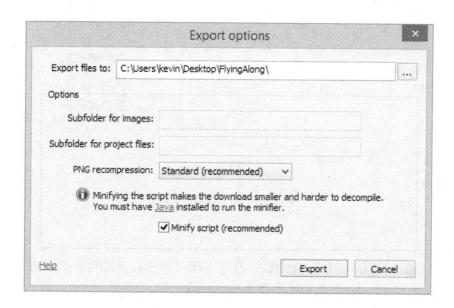

Minify script is an option that requires you to have the proper Java version installed on your development station. The installer cannot configure Java for you so you must do this yourself. It is OPTIONAL if file size is not much of a concern to you.

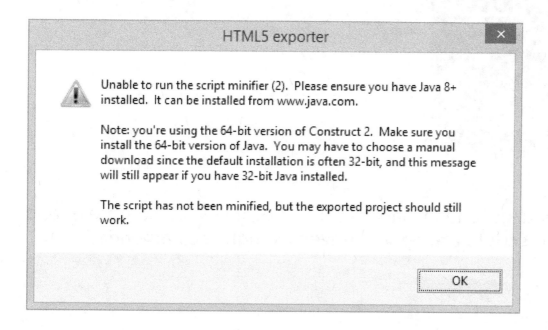

You can choose the possible window mode. Kiosk mode is full screen.

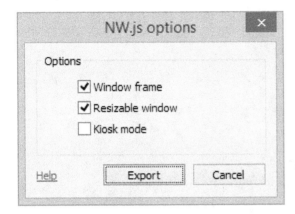

By default, NW.js will produce 5 sets of results for you:

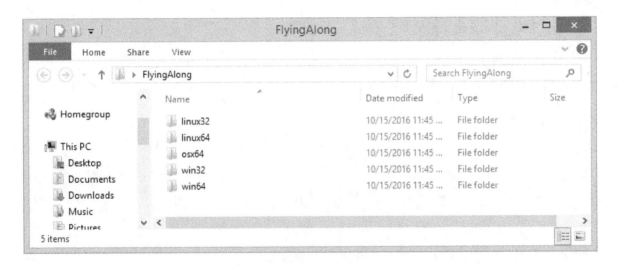

For Windows, win32 is the most compatible one since it will run under Win64 as well (Win64 won't run on a 32bit Windows). The files produced has an executable known as NW. You can click to run the game through it - no separate installation process is required.

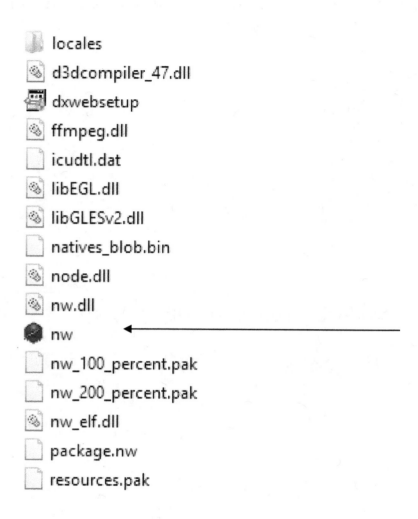

locales
d3dcompiler_47.dll
dxwebsetup
ffmpeg.dll
icudtl.dat
libEGL.dll
libGLESv2.dll
natives_blob.bin
node.dll
nw.dll
nw ←
nw_100_percent.pak
nw_200_percent.pak
nw_elf.dll
package.nw
resources.pak

For the latest content update, please visit:

http://gameengines.net/

Please email your questions and comments to

editor@HobbyPRESS.net.